High Fibre
COOKING

High Fibre
C O O K I N G

A N N E   S H E A S B Y

Photography by David Jordan

southwater

This edition is published by Southwater

Southwater is an imprint of
Anness Publishing Limited
Hermes House
88–89 Blackfriars Road
London SE1 8HA
tel. 020 7401 2077
fax 020 7633 9499

Distributed in the UK by
The Manning Partnership
251–253 London Road East
Batheaston
Bath BA1 7RL
tel. 01225 852 727
fax 01225 852 852

Distributed in the USA by
Anness Publishing Inc.
27 West 20th Street
Suite 504
New York
NY 10011
fax 212 807 6813

Distributed in Australia by
Sandstone Publishing
Unit 1
360 Norton Street
Leichhardt
New South Wales 2040
tel. 02 9560 7888
fax 02 9560 7488

1 3 5 7 9 10 8 6 4 2

Publisher: Joanna Lorenz
Senior Cookery Editor: Linda Fraser
Project editor: Anne Hildyard
Designer: Lilian Lindblom
Photographer: David Jordan
Stylist: Judy Williams
For all recipes, quantities are given in both metric and imperial measures,
and where appropriate, measures are also given in standard cups and spoons.
Follow one set, but not a mixture, because they are not interchangeable.

Previously published as Step-by-step: *High Fibre Cookbook*

CONTENTS

INTRODUCTION

Dietary fiber, or roughage, as it used to be known, plays an important part in a healthy, balanced diet, and most of us need to increase our daily intake. Dietary fiber is very important for maintaining a healthy digestive system. In the US, we eat about 11 grams of fiber a day, although it is recommended that our daily intake be 20–30 grams.

Dietary fiber is more accurately referred to as non-starch polysaccharides (NSP), of which there are two main types: soluble and insoluble. Both are important as part of a healthy, low-fat, high-fiber diet. It is easy to increase the fiber content in your diet without changing your eating patterns very much, and there are lots of delicious ways of adding natural fiber to your meals, rather than merely adding bran to your food.

This book contains many tempting and delicious recipes, all full of nutrients and high in dietary fiber. It explains the benefits of following a healthy, balanced diet high in fiber and suggests ways to increase the fiber content of your diet by making a few simple changes. It also gives useful information on the fiber content of foods.

Pantry Items and Ingredients

Breakfast Cereals

A wide variety of breakfast cereals is available. Whole-wheat or whole-grain varieties are the best choice for fiber—preferably those that are also low in fat and sugar. Try using whole-wheat breakfast cereals when making granola bars and pancakes, crisp toppings and cheesecake crusts, in coffee cakes, meat loaves and burgers and when coating foods.

Brown Rice

There are many varieties of brown rice available, including long, medium and short grain, basmati, texmati and jasmine, as well as boil-in-the bag brown rice for convenience.

The flavor of brown rice is quite nutty, and because the rice undergoes only minor milling, the bran layer is retained, making it higher in fiber, vitamins and minerals than white rice. Rice is also low in fat. Cooking time for brown rice is about 35 minutes, during which time it expands and increases by up to three times in volume. Allow at least $^1/_3$ cup uncooked rice per person.

Canned Beans, Peas and Lentils

There are many kinds of canned beans, peas and lentils available in supermarkets. Varieties include black-eyed peas, lima beans, chickpeas, cannellini, lentils, peas and red kidney beans. Red and green canned beans are very nutritious and high in fiber and are convenient to use, so it is well worth having a few cans in your cupboard. They are also low in fat and high in protein, vitamins and minerals.

Add dried beans to recipes for dishes such as salads, soups, pâtés and hamburgers to boost the fiber content. Reduce the amount of meat used in a recipe and replace it with some cooked legumes. Mashed, cooked beans are a good basis for dips, served with a selection of crunchy vegetable crudités.

Dried Beans, Peas and Lentils

There are many varieties of dried beans available. When buying, choose dried beans that are plump, bright and clear in color and avoid broken, shriveled or dusty beans. Beans should be stored in a cool, dry place in an airtight container and used within one year.

Many dried beans need to be soaked in water before cooking and boiled for a period until tender. The older the beans are, the longer they will take to cook. Salt should be added at the end of the cooking time. Some beans, such as red kidney beans, contain a toxic substance known as hemagglutinin, which can lead to acute gastroenteritis if it is not destroyed by adequate cooking. These beans need to be boiled rapidly for at least 10 minutes to destroy the hemagglutinin, then simmered until they are tender.

Dried Fruit

A good selection of dried fruit is available, including apples, apricots, bananas, currants, figs, kiwi fruit, lychees, mangoes, papayas, peaches, pears, pineapple, prunes and dark and golden raisins. They are very versatile and can be used in both sweet and savory dishes. Dried fruit is also a useful source of dietary fiber and is low in fat, so it makes a delicious, healthy snack when you feel the need to nibble. Add dried fruit to your breakfast cereals, granola or hot cereal and use it in cake, scone, biscuit, dessert and muffin recipes.

Nuts

Nuts are a useful source of dietary fiber and have many uses in a wide selection of sweet and savory dishes. They also make a tasty snack, but as they are high in fat and calories, eat them only in small quantities. Nuts with a good source of dietary fiber include almonds, brazil nuts, hazelnuts, peanuts, pecans, pistachios and walnuts. Some nuts, such as almonds and hazelnuts, are also a good source of vitamin E. Add nuts to salads, cakes and breads, biscuits, desserts, stuffings, coatings and stir-fries.

Oats and Oatmeal

Oats and oatmeal are valuable sources of soluble fiber, which is absorbed into the body and is thought to help reduce high levels of blood cholesterol. Oats and oatmeal come in a variety of types, including steel-cut oats, rolled oats, quick-cooking oats and instant oatmeal. Use them in muesli, oatcakes, mixed with flour for breads and rolls, cakes and small cakes such as gingerbread and pancakes, and crispy toppings. Oats also make a good thickener for soups and sauces.

Seeds

Seeds such as sesame, sunflower and pumpkin are all good sources of dietary fiber. They can be eaten on their own as a snack or added to recipes for salads, stir-fries, stuffings, cakes and breads, coatings, muesli, cookies and crackers. Seeds also contain vitamins and minerals but are high in fat and calories, so they should be eaten in small quantities.

Spices

These age-old flavorings from all over the world are available in a variety of forms – whole, ground or blended – in a vast range of different types. Each spice has its unique flavor and aroma, and with a single spice or a simple blend of spices, everyday dishes can be enhanced and transformed. Spices are invaluable pantry items, and many can be used in both sweet and savory dishes.

Spices should be kept in airtight, tinted glass containers and stored in a cool, dark cupboard. Ground spices should be used within six months and whole spices within a year, so it is better to buy them in small quantities. Because freshly ground spices provide the best flavor and aroma, it is well worth investing in a small mortar and pestle so that you can grind your own.

Sugars and Honey
There is no caloric difference between white (refined) and brown (unrefined) sugar, but the flavors vary. Many of the recipes in this book use light brown sugar, but other sugars, such as raw sugar or dark brown sugar, if available, can be used in its place.

Honey is also used in sweet and savory dishes, and clear honey is specified in most recipes. However, other varieties can be substituted for a change, chosen from the many types and flavors available. Honey is a little sweeter than sugar, so often a smaller amount is needed in a recipe.

Wheat Bran
Natural wheat bran is the hard outer layer or casing that surrounds the wheat grain; it is therefore high in fiber. Other brans, such as rice bran, oat bran and soy bran, are also available, but wheat bran is the most common.

Bran is a useful ingredient and can be added to many recipes to enrich breads, cakes and cereals.

Avoid simply adding or sprinkling plain bran on your food to increase your fiber intake. It is no substitute for getting fiber from food itself.

Whole-wheat Flour
Whole-wheat flour is 100% flour that has been milled from the whole of the wheat grain. "Whole" means that the grain has not had the bran, vitamins and minerals refined out – in other words, it has had nothing added or removed, so it contains all the nutrients. Whole-wheat flour is coarser than white flour and is available in several types, including plain and self-rising. It is very versatile and can be used in many dishes that traditionally specify white flour, including cakes, muffins, breads, pastry, cookies and crackers. It makes a good thickener for sauces and can be used to coat foods. A mixture of half whole-wheat and half white flour can be used in recipes where a lighter flour is required.

Whole-wheat Cookies and Crackers
Whole-wheat cookies and high fiber crackers make good pantry standbys for a healthy, high-fiber snack. Try serving savory varieties with a selection of cheeses, or spread with low-fat spread, honey or reduced-sugar jam for a tasty snack. When crushed, sweet whole-wheat cookies are good for cheesecake crusts and crunchy toppings for fruity desserts. Whole-wheat cereal bars are also available and make a good snack, but beware of added fat and sugar, and eat them as a treat rather than regularly.

Whole-wheat Pasta
Dried whole-wheat pasta is a good source of dietary fiber and carbohydrate, is low in fat and contains some B vitamins. It is an essential pantry item and is a great basis for many quick and easy nutritious meals. Pasta is very versatile and can be used in many dishes, including salads, pasta casseroles and filled pasta, which can be topped with low-fat sauces.

Allow 4–8 ounces (1–2 cups) pasta per serving for a main course and 2–4 ounces (½–1 cup) per person for a first course. Dried whole-wheat pasta takes about 12 minutes to cook.

Fresh Foods and Ingredients

Fresh Beans and Peas

There are many varieties of fresh beans and peas available, including peas, fava beans and Italian green beans and more unusual ones such as Chinese long beans, black-eyed peas and lima beans.

Fresh corn on the cob and baby corn are also popular, as are snow peas, sugar-snap peas and green beans.

All are good sources of dietary fiber and contain other nutrients, including vitamins and minerals. Beans and peas are very versatile and can be used in many dishes including salads, stir-fries, casseroles, pasta sauces, soups and curries. Some varieties, such as sugar-snap peas and snow peas, can be eaten either raw or cooked.

Fresh Fruit

Fresh fruit plays an important part in a healthy, balanced, high-fiber diet. Choose fruits that contain useful amounts of fiber, such as apples, pears and bananas, berries such as raspberries, blackberries and gooseberries, and guava, mangoes, oranges, peaches and pears.

Fruits are very versatile and can be enjoyed raw or cooked, on their own or as part of a recipe. They are also good sources of vitamins and minerals, particularly vitamin C. A piece of fresh fruit makes a quick and easy nutritious snack at any time of the day. Try topping whole-wheat breakfast cereals with some fruit, such as raspberries, for a tasty and nutritious start to the day.

Fresh Herbs

In cooking, herbs are used mainly for their flavoring and seasoning properties, as well as for adding color and texture. They have a great deal to offer: by simply adding a single herb or a combination of herbs to foods, everyday dishes can be transformed into delicious meals.

Herbs are also very low in fat and calories, and those such as parsley provide a useful balance of vitamins and minerals. Many people grow their own herbs; a wide selection is also available in supermarkets, vegetable markets and local groceries.

Potatoes

Potatoes are one of the most commonly eaten vegetables in the world and are valuable in terms of nutrition. They are high in carbohydrate, low in fat and contain some vitamin C and dietary fiber. Potatoes contain more dietary fiber when eaten with their skins on. Wash old and new potatoes thoroughly and cook them with their skins on – for example, baked, boiled and roasted. The flavor will be just as delicious, and you will be getting extra fiber.

Potatoes are very versatile and are used in many dishes. Mashed potatoes (with their skins left on, of course!) make an ideal topping for savory pies and casseroles. For roast potatoes, use a minimum amount

of oil, and if you need to make french fries, leave the skins on and cut the slices thickly using a knife. With baked and mashed potatoes, avoid adding high-fat butter, sour cream or cheese and instead use skim milk, low-fat hard cheese and herbs to add flavor.

Fresh Vegetables

Fresh vegetables, like fresh fruit, play an important part in a healthy, balanced diet. We are now encouraged to eat at least five portions of fruit and vegetables each day for a healthy diet. Vegetables are nutritious and are valuable sources of vitamins and minerals, some being especially rich in vitamins A, C and E. Vegetables also contain some dietary fiber; those that are particularly good sources include broccoli, Brussels sprouts, cabbage, carrots, fennel, okra, parsnips, spinach, chard, collards and corn.

Vegetables are also very versatile, and many can be eaten either raw or cooked. Add vegetables to dishes such as soups, stews, casseroles, stir-fries, salads, hamburgers and meat loaves, or simply serve them on their own, raw or lightly cooked and tossed in a little lemon juice.

Whole-wheat Baked Goods

Baked goods such as whole-wheat pita breads, scones, muffins and cupcakes make a good high-fiber snack or treat. Choose whole-wheat or whole-grain varieties whenever possible, or bake your own at home using whole-wheat flour and adding extra dried fruit. Serve bagels, scones or muffins plain or with a little low-fat

spread, honey or reduced-sugar jam for a delicious, filling snack.

Whole-wheat Bread

Bread has been an important part of the diet in many countries for thousands of years, and nowadays continues to contribute to a healthy, balanced diet. Bread is available in many varieties and is a good source of carbohydrates as well as being low in fat. It also contains some calcium, iron and B vitamins, and whole-wheat varieties are high in fiber.

Make delicious sandwiches and toasted sandwiches using whole-wheat bread and low-fat fillings. Use whole-wheat bread crumbs in recipes for stuffings, coatings and toppings, and serve thick slices of whole-wheat bread at mealtimes for a filling, healthy and high-fiber accompaniment to many dishes.

High Fiber Food Charts

The information shows dietary fiber per 3½ ounces, unless otherwise stated.

BREADS	FIBER (g)
brown bread	3.5
brown bread (1 medium slice)	1.3
multigrain bread	4.3
multigrain bread (1 medium slice)	1.5
white pita bread	2.2
white pita bread (1 medium pita)	1.4
whole-wheat pita bread	6.4
whole-wheat pita (1 medium pita)	4.1
rye bread	4.4
rye bread (1 average slice)	1.1
white bread	1.5
white bread (1 medium slice)	0.5
white bread with added fiber	3.1
white bread with added fiber (1 medium slice)	1.1
whole-wheat bread	5.8
whole-wheat bread (1 medium slice)	2.1

FLOURS AND GRAINS	FIBER (g)
wheat bran	36.4
oatmeal	6.8
rolled oats	7.0
wheat flour, brown	6.4
wheat flour, white	3.1
wheat flour, whole-wheat	9.0
wheat germ	15.6
brown rice, boiled	0.8
white rice, boiled	0.1
white spaghetti, boiled	1.2
whole-wheat spaghetti, boiled	3.5

BREAKFAST CEREALS	FIBER (g)
All-bran	24.5
All-bran (30g serving)	7.4
Branflakes	13.0
Branflakes (30g serving)	3.9
Cornflakes	0.9
Cornflakes (30g serving)	0.3
Frosted Flakes	0.6
Frosted Flakes (30g serving)	0.2
Fruit 'n' fiber	7.0
Fruit 'n' fiber (30g serving)	2.1
muesli – Swiss style	6.4
muesli – Swiss style (30g serving)	1.9
muesli – no added sugar	7.6
muesli – no added sugar (30g)	2.3
porridge	0.8
porridge (30g serving)	0.2
Puffed Wheat	5.6
Puffed Wheat (30g serving)	1.7
Raisin Bran	10.0
Raisin Bran (30g serving)	3.0
Rice Krispies	0.7
Rice Krispies (30g serving)	0.2
Shredded Wheat	9.8
Shredded Wheat (30g serving)	2.9

COOKIES	FIBER (g)
cracker	2.2
cracker (each)	0.2
crispbread, rye	11.7
crispbread, rye (each)	1.2
crispbread, high fiber	17.9
crispbread, high fiber (each)	1.8
graham cracker, plain	2.2
graham cracker, plain (each)	0.3
oatcake	5.9
oatcake (each)	0.8
shortbread finger	1.9
shortbread finger (each)	0.2

CAKES	FIBER (g)
fruitcake, rich	1.7
fruitcake, rich (per slice)	1.2
fruitcake, whole-wheat	2.4
fruitcake, whole-wheat (per slice)	1.7
sponge cake	0.9
sponge cake (per slice)	0.5
muffin, plain	2.0
muffin, plain (each)	1.4
muffin, bran	7.7
muffin, bran (each)	5.4
scone, plain	1.9
scone, plain (each)	0.9
scone, whole-wheat	5.2
scone, whole-wheat (each)	

PASTRY	FIBER (g)
unsweetened pie crust, cooked	2.2
whole-wheat pie crust, cooked	6.3

The information presented in these tables has been adapted from McCance and Widdowson's *The Composition of Foods*, 5th Edition, and relevant supplements. Data are reproduced with the kind permission of The Royal Society of Chemistry and the Controller of Her Majesty's Stationery Office.

BEANS, PEAS AND LENTILS	FIBER (g)
baked beans in tomato sauce	3.7
chickpeas, canned	4.1
fava beans, boiled	6.5
fava beans, canned	4.6
green beans, boiled	4.1
lentils, brown and green, boiled	3.8
lentils, red split, boiled	1.9
peas, boiled	5.1
red kidney beans, canned	6.2
runner beans, boiled	1.9
snow peas, boiled	2.2

VEGETABLES	FIBER (g)
broccoli, boiled	2.3
Brussels sprouts, boiled	3.1
cabbage, raw	2.4
cabbage, boiled	1.8
carrots, raw	2.4
carrots, boiled	2.5
celeriac, boiled	3.2
collard greens, boiled	2.6
corn kernels, canned	1.4
fennel, boiled	2.3
leeks, boiled	1.7
okra, boiled	3.6
onion, raw	1.4
parsnips, boiled	4.7
potatoes, baked, flesh and skin	2.7
potatoes, boiled	1.2
spinach, raw	2.1
spinach, boiled	2.1
squash, baked	2.1
sweet potatoes, boiled	2.3
turnip, boiled	1.9

FRUIT	FIBER (g)
(Figures given are for raw fruit unless otherwise stated)	
apple, eating	1.8
apple, eating (each)	1.8
apricots, dried	6.3
avocado	3.4
banana	1.1
banana (each)	1.1
blackberries	3.1
dates, dried	3.4
figs, dried	6.9
gooseberries, stewed, no sugar	2.0
grapefruit	1.3
grapefruit (half)	1.0
guava	3.7
kiwi fruit	1.9
kiwi fruit (each)	1.1
mango	2.6
orange	1.7
orange (each)	2.7
passion fruit	3.3
passion fruit (each)	0.5
peach	1.5
peach (each)	1.7
peaches, dried	7.3
pear	2.2
pear (each)	3.3
pears, dried	8.3
pineapple	1.2
pineapple, dried	8.1
prunes	5.7
raisins	2.0
raspberries	2.5

NUTS AND SEEDS	FIBER (g)
almonds	7.4
brazil nuts	4.3
chestnuts	4.1
dessicated coconut	13.7
hazelnuts	6.5
peanuts	6.2
pecans	4.7
pistachio nuts	6.1
pumpkin seeds	5.3
sesame seeds	7.9
sunflower seeds	6.0
walnuts	3.5

High Fiber Diet for Life

Changing to a diet that is higher in dietary fiber is simple to do but should be done gradually. Sudden changes to your normal eating patterns may upset the digestive system.

Dietary fiber, or non-starch polysaccharides (NSP), are divided into two main types – soluble fiber and insoluble fiber. Soluble fiber dissolves in water to form a soft, gooey liquid or gel that can be fermented by bacteria and absorbed by the body. Soluble fiber is found in foods such as oats, oat bran, oatmeal, dried beans, peas and lentils and in some fruit and vegetables such as oranges, bananas, corn and green leafy vegetables.

Insoluble fiber cannot be digested by the body and passes through and out of the body unchanged. Insoluble fiber is found in cereal-based foods such as whole-wheat bread, whole-wheat pasta, brown rice, whole-wheat and bran breakfast cereals, and the skins of some fruit and vegetables.

Both soluble and insoluble fiber are important to maintain a healthy digestive system. Low intakes of dietary fiber are associated with an increased risk of bowel disease as well as disorders such as constipation. Fiber, particularly cereal (insoluble) fiber, helps to regulate bowel function and helps to prevent constipation

and other intestinal disorders such as hemorrhoids and diverticular disease.

Dietary fiber is also thought to be protective against diseases such as large bowel cancer and is sometimes successful in treating irritable bowel syndrome. It may also help to lower the rate of colon cancer. Research also shows that small amounts of soluble fiber are absorbed into the bloodstream, and this is thought to help lower high cholesterol levels in the blood.

It is very important to drink plenty of nonalcoholic fluids as part of a healthy diet – at least 8 glasses a day (preferably water) – but especially when the diet is high in fiber. Undigested fiber absorbs and holds fluid in the gut to form soft and bulky stools that move along the bowel more quickly. Suitable fluids include water, some fruit juice, low-fat milk, some coffee and tea. If insufficient liquid is taken in, conditions such as constipation may be aggravated.

There are many simple ways of introducing more fiber into your diet, but simply adding bran to your food is no substitute for getting fiber from food itself. Wheat bran can be an irritant and it is high in substances called phytates, which can interfere with the absorption of essential minerals such as iron, calcium and zinc.

It is important to obtain a mixture of both soluble and insoluble fiber from a variety of

foods that are naturally good sources of fiber, rather than taking supplements. By choosing foods that are naturally high in fiber, you will benefit from the other important nutrients, such as vitamins and minerals, in those foods. For example, simply switching from white to whole-wheat bread, white pasta to whole-wheat pasta, white rice to brown rice or choosing whole-wheat breakfast cereals are easy ways of gradually introducing more fiber into your diet. Serve dishes with slices of whole-wheat bread, cooked brown rice or whole-wheat pasta to add extra fiber and flavor to mealtimes.

Many foods that are higher in fiber also tend to be filling, bulky and lower in calories. Weight watchers and dieters are able to fill up on high-fiber, starchy foods such as whole-grain cereals, bread, pasta and rice, and as a result leave less room for refined foods, which tend to be higher in fat and sugar.

Nowadays, most foods carry a label with a nutritional information panel that follows a standard format for the type of information it includes. A figure for the dietary fiber content will be given on such a panel, and this can be useful to get an idea of how much fiber different foods contain. Ideally, we should aim to eat between 20 and 30 grams of dietary fiber per day.

QUICK AND EASY WAYS TO INCREASE FIBER IN YOUR DIET

- Choose whole-wheat, whole-grain, high-fiber, brown or granary bread in place of white bread.

- Choose whole-wheat pita bread, rolls, muffins, scones and bagels in place of white.

- Choose whole-wheat pasta in place of white pasta.

- Choose brown rice in place of white rice. Mixtures of brown and wild rice are also available and offer a tasty alternative.

- Use whole-wheat flour in place of white flour. Alternatively, use a mixture of half white flour and half whole-wheat flour.

- Choose whole-wheat breakfast cereals that are naturally high in fiber rather than adding plain bran to cereals.

- Make your own high-fiber muesli by combining oats, bran flakes, wheat germ, dried fruit, nuts and seeds, and serve topped with fresh fruit such as sliced bananas or raspberries.

- Add dried fruit such as raisins, chopped dried pears or peaches to breakfast cereals or porridge.

- Include a food from the cereal group (bread, pasta, rice, cereals) at every meal, if possible.

- Choose high-fiber crackers, crispbreads and cookies rather than plain ones.

- Choose dried-bean dishes as a change from meat or fish-based ones.

- Reduce the amount of meat used in a recipe and replace it with some cooked dried peas, beans or lentils. Many varieties of fresh, frozen and canned dried beans are available that are convenient and easy to use.

- Extend soups by adding cooked dried beans, peas or lentils.

- Add cooked dried beans, nuts or seeds to salads for extra fiber, color and flavor.

- Avoid peeling fruit and vegetables whenever possible, but wash them thoroughly before eating or cooking.

- Leave skins on potatoes, especially baked potatoes, boiled potatoes and even roast potatoes.

- When making vegetable soups and sauces, leave the vegetables in pieces, or if puréeing, do not pass the mixture through a sieve, because much of the valuable fiber will be discarded.

- Add grated root vegetables such as potatoes or parsnips to casseroles, lasagne, shepherd's pie, sauces and stews.

- Use whole-wheat bread crumbs in recipes such as stuffings, coatings and toppings.

- Use whole-wheat breakfast cereals in baking. Try muesli bars for toppings or crisp coatings, cheesecake crusts, and in meat loaves and hamburgers.

- Add dried fruit such as raisins and chopped dried apricots to recipes for cakes, scones and muffins.

- Snack on fresh or dried fruit or whole-wheat cookies, oatcakes, cereal bars, fruit cake, whole-wheat bagels and muffins.

- Some nuts and seeds contain a good amount of fiber and make a tasty snack or addition to a recipe, but use sparingly, as they are also high in fat and calories.

- For dessert, choose fresh or dried fruit salad or compote, whole-wheat bread pudding, or whole-wheat fruit crisps or fruit cakes.

- For toasted sandwiches, use whole-wheat bread in place of white bread.

- Use leftover cooked brown rice for rice salads and stuffings.

- Use leftover cooked whole-wheat pasta for pasta salads.

- Choose ready-made sandwiches made from whole-wheat bread with a low calorie or reduced-fat filling. Better still, if you have time, make your own high-fiber sandwich to pack up and take to work.

High Fiber Meal Comparisons and Menus

There are many easy ways of increasing the fiber content of everyday meals by making one or two simple changes. These changes will increase the dietary fiber content of your meals considerably, and you will hardly notice the difference.

Six pairs of everyday meals are illustrated. In each case a couple of simple changes have been made to make them higher in natural dietary fiber. You can see how quick and easy it is to increase the fiber content of your meals markedly.

For the following meal comparisons, the dietary fiber content in grams (g) of each meal is shown per typical serving of the meal.

FRESH TOMATO SOUP

Dietary fiber content = 3.09g

FRESH TOMATO, LENTIL AND ONION SOUP

The quantity of tomatoes has been reduced slightly and lentils have been added.
Dietary fiber content = 4.27g

CHILI CON CARNE SERVED ON A BED OF BOILED WHITE RICE

Dietary fiber content = 4.59g

CHILI CON CARNE SERVED ON A BED OF BOILED BROWN RICE

The quantity of meat (lean ground beef) in the chili has been reduced slightly and extra cooked red kidney beans have been added.
Dietary fiber content = 8.29g

CHEESE AND TOMATO PIZZA WITH WHITE CRUST

Dietary fiber content = 1.99g

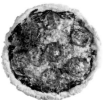

ZUCCHINI, CORN AND PLUM TOMATO WHOLE-WHEAT PIZZA

Whole-wheat flour was used in place of white flour for the dough. Mushrooms, zucchini, onion and corn were added to the topping.
Dietary fiber content = 4.93g

WHITE PASTA SALAD WITH PEPPERS AND MUSHROOMS·

Dietary fiber content = 5.82g

ROAST PEPPER AND WILD MUSHROOM PASTA SALAD

Whole-wheat pasta was used in place of white pasta and raisins used in place of cherry tomatoes.
Dietary fiber content = 9.37g

HOMEMADE COLESLAW

Dietary fiber content = 2.92g

CARROT, RAISIN AND APRICOT COLESLAW

The quantity of cabbage has been reduced slightly and celery, raisins and dried apricots have been added.
Dietary fiber content = 4.25g

APPLE CRISP MADE USING WHITE FLOUR

Dietary fiber content = 3.86g

PEACH AND RASPBERRY CRISP

A mixture of whole-wheat flour and rolled oats was used in place of white flour for the crisp topping and peaches and raspberries in place of apples for the base.
Dietary fiber content = 5.22g

TECHNIQUES

Puréeing Soup

1 Allow the cooked soup to cool slightly, then ladle it into a blender or food processor.

2 Process the mixture until smooth. If there is a large quantity of soup, blend or purée it in a couple of batches.

3 Rinse the saucepan, then pour the blended soup back into it. Adjust the seasoning and reheat the soup gently before serving.

Peeling Tomatoes

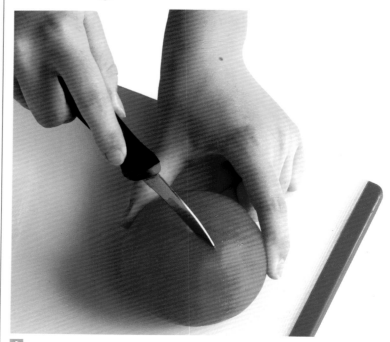

1 Using a sharp knife, cut a small cross in the base of each tomato.

2 Place the tomatoes in a bowl and cover them with boiling water. Leave them for 30 seconds, then, using a slotted spoon, transfer them to a bowl of cold water.

3 Remove the tomatoes from the water and peel off the skins. Slice or chop the tomatoes and use as required in the recipe.

Cooking Long grain Brown Rice

1 Put the rice in a large saucepan and cover with plenty of boiling water (about 5¾ cups of water to 9 ounces rice).

2 Stir, bring back to a boil and simmer, uncovered, for about 35 minutes, until al dente (tender but firm to the bite).

3 Drain the rice through a sieve, then rinse it with fresh boiling water.

Chopping Dried Fruit

Use scissors to cut up dried fruit such as apricots, prunes, pears and peaches.

1 Using a pair of clean kitchen scissors, cut a piece of dried fruit (pear in this instance) into three pieces lengthwise.

2 Cut all the dried fruit lengthwise into strips.

3 Snip each length into small, even pieces and use as required in recipes. A sharp knife and a cutting board may be used in place of the scissors, but scissors are the quickest and easiest way of chopping larger pieces of dried fruit.

Making Whole-wheat Pastry

1 Put flour and salt in a bowl and add shortening. Rub shortening into the flour with your fingertips until the mixture resembles bread crumbs.

2 Using a round-bladed knife, keep stirring in small amounts of cold water until the mixture begins to stick together in lumps.

3 Collect the dough together and knead lightly to form a smooth, soft ball. Wrap in waxed paper or foil and let rest in the refrigerator for 30 minutes before rolling out and using as required.

Preventing Fruit Discoloration

Use this method for bananas, apples and pears.

1 Choose firm, ripe fruit (bananas in this instance). Peel, slice and put the fruit into a bowl.

2 Sprinkle lemon juice liberally all over the fruit.

3 Remove the fruit from the bowl using a slotted spoon to drain off any excess lemon juice and use as required as soon as possible. Discard any remaining lemon juice.

Lining a Pan

Segmenting an Orange

1 Cut the top and bottom off the orange and stand it on a board. Using a small serrated knife, cut the peel off the fruit, following the shape as closely as possible.

2 Trim around the orange again to remove all remaining pith.

1 Place the pan on waxed paper and draw around the bottom of it. Cut out the shape just inside the line.

2 Wrap a piece of waxed paper around the outside of the pan and cut it 2 inches longer and 1 inch wider.

3 Fold one long edge over by 1 inch and make diagonal cuts at regular intervals up to the fold. Grease the pan lightly to help the paper stick to it. Place the long strip around the inside of the pan so that the fringed edge sits on the bottom. Lay the round piece of paper on top.

3 Holding the orange over a bowl to catch any juice, cut close to the membrane in each orange segment and lift out the slices.

Spicy Chickpea and Bacon Soup

This is a tasty mixture of chickpeas and bacon flavored with a subtle mix of spices.

NUTRITIONAL NOTES

PER PORTION:

CALORIES 207 PROTEIN 15.56g
FAT 7.28g SATURATED FAT 1.43g
CARBOHYDRATE 22.40g
FIBER 4.82g ADDED SUGAR 0.02g
SODIUM 1.17g

Serves 4–6

INGREDIENTS

2 teaspoons sunflower oil
1 onion, chopped
2 garlic cloves, crushed
1 teaspoon each garam masala and
  ground coriander, cumin
  and turmeric
½ teaspoon chili powder
2 tablespoons all-purpose
  whole-wheat flour
2½ cups vegetable stock
1 can (14 ounces) chopped tomatoes
1 can (14 ounces) chickpeas, rinsed
  and drained
6 slices smoked Canadian bacon
salt and ground black pepper
cilantro sprigs, to garnish

1 Heat the oil in a large saucepan. Add the onion and garlic and cook for 5 minutes, stirring occasionally.

2 Add the spices and flour and cook for 1 minute, stirring.

3 Gradually add the stock, stirring constantly, then add the tomatoes and chickpeas.

sunflower oil

garlic

garam masala

ground coriander

onion

ground cumin

ground turmeric

chili powder

whole-wheat flour

vegetable stock

chopped tomatoes

chickpeas

Canadian bacon

salt

black pepper

cilantro

4 Bring to a boil, stirring, then cover and simmer for 25 minutes, stirring occasionally.

COOK'S TIP

Use other canned beans such as red kidney beans or cannellini beans in place of the chickpeas.

5 Meanwhile, broil the bacon for 2–3 minutes on each side.

6 Dice the bacon, then stir into the soup. Season to taste, reheat gently until piping hot and ladle into soup bowls to serve. Garnish each with a cilantro sprig and serve immediately.

Fresh Tomato, Lentil and Onion Soup

This wholesome soup is delicious served with thick slices of whole-wheat or multigrain bread.

Serves 4–6

INGREDIENTS
2 teaspoons sunflower oil
1 large onion, chopped
2 stalks celery, chopped
1 cup split red lentils
2 large tomatoes, peeled and
  coarsely chopped
4 cups vegetable stock
2 teaspoons dried *herbes
  de Provence*
salt and ground black pepper
chopped fresh parsley, to garnish

sunflower oil

onion

celery

*split red
lentils*

tomatoes

herbes de
Provence

*vegetable
stock*

salt

black pepper

NUTRITIONAL NOTES
PER PORTION:

CALORIES 202 PROTEIN 12.40g
FAT 3.07g SATURATED FAT 0.38g
CARBOHYDRATE 33.34g
FIBER 4.27g ADDED SUGAR 0.04g
SODIUM 0.54g

1 Heat the oil in a large saucepan. Add the onion and celery and cook for 5 minutes, stirring occasionally. Add the lentils and cook for 1 minute.

2 Stir in the tomatoes, stock, herbs and seasoning. Cover, bring to a boil and simmer for about 20 minutes, stirring occasionally.

3 When the lentils are cooked and tender, set the soup aside to cool slightly.

4 Purée in a blender or food processor until smooth. Adjust the seasoning, return to the saucepan and reheat gently until piping hot. Ladle into soup bowls to serve and garnish each with chopped parsley.

Pea, Leek and Broccoli Soup

A delicious and nutritious soup, ideal for warming those chilly winter evenings.

Serves 4–6

INGREDIENTS
1 onion, chopped
2 cups trimmed, sliced leeks
8 ounces unpeeled potatoes, diced
3¾ cups vegetable stock or
 vegetable bouillon cube and water
1 bay leaf
2 cups broccoli florets
1½ cups frozen peas
2–3 tablespoons chopped
 fresh parsley, plus leaves
 to garnish
salt and ground black pepper

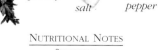

onion *leeks*

potatoes

vegetable stock *bay leaf*

broccoli *peas*

parsley *salt* *black pepper*

NUTRITIONAL NOTES

PER PORTION:

CALORIES 125 PROTEIN 8.11g
FAT 1.92g SATURATED FAT 0.26g
CARBOHYDRATE 19.94g
FIBER 6.31g ADDED SUGAR 0.04g
SODIUM 0.52g

1 Put the onion, leeks, potatoes, stock and bay leaf in a large saucepan and stir together. Cover, bring to a boil and simmer for 10 minutes, stirring.

2 Add the broccoli and peas, cover, return to a boil and simmer for another 10 minutes, stirring occasionally.

COOK'S TIP

If you prefer, cut the vegetables finely and leave the soup chunky rather than puréeing it.

3 Set aside to cool slightly and remove and discard the bay leaf. Purée in a blender or food processor until smooth.

4 Add the parsley, season to taste and process briefly. Return to the saucepan and reheat gently until piping hot. Ladle into soup bowls and garnish with parsley leaves.

Curried Celery Soup

An unusual combination of flavors, this warming soup is excellent served with warm whole-wheat bread rolls or whole-wheat pita bread.

NUTRITIONAL NOTES

PER PORTION:

CALORIES 102 PROTEIN 3.72g
FAT 2.93g SATURATED FAT 0.25g
CARBOHYDRATE 16.11g
FIBER 4.44g ADDED SUGAR 0.04g
SODIUM 0.62g

Serves 4–6

INGREDIENTS
2 teaspoons olive oil
1 onion, chopped
1 leek, washed and sliced
1½ pounds celery, chopped,
  leaves reserved
1 tablespoon curry powder
8 ounces unpeeled potatoes,
  washed and diced
4 cups vegetable stock or vegetable
  bouillon cube and water
1 bouquet garni
2 tablespoons chopped fresh
  mixed herbs
salt
celery seeds and leaves, to garnish

olive oil

onion

leek

celery

curry powder

potatoes

vegetable stock

bouquet garni

fresh mixed herbs

salt

celery seeds

1 Heat the oil in a large saucepan. Add the onion, leek and celery, cover and cook gently for 10 minutes, stirring occasionally.

2 Add the curry powder and cook for 2 minutes, stirring occasionally.

3 Add the potatoes, stock and bouquet garni, cover and bring to a boil. Simmer for 20 minutes or until the vegetables are tender.

4 Remove and discard the bouquet garni and set the soup aside to cool slightly.

5 Purée in a blender or food processor until smooth.

6 Add the mixed herbs, season to taste and process briefly. Return to the saucepan and reheat gently until piping hot. Ladle into soup bowls and garnish each with a sprinkling of celery seeds and some celery leaves.

COOK'S TIP

For a tasty change, use celeriac and sweet potatoes in place of celery and standard potatoes.

Mushroom and Bean Pâté

A light and tasty pâté, delicious served on whole-wheat bread or toast for an appetizer or a suppertime snack.

Serves 12

INGREDIENTS
6 cups mushrooms, sliced
1 onion, chopped
2 garlic cloves, crushed
1 red bell pepper, seeded and diced
2 tablespoons vegetable stock
2 tablespoons dry white wine
1 can (14 ounces) red kidney
  beans, rinsed and drained
1 egg, beaten
1 cup fresh whole-wheat
  bread crumbs
1 tablespoon chopped fresh thyme
1 tablespoon chopped fresh
  rosemary
salt and ground black pepper
lettuce and tomatoes, to garnish

1 Preheat the oven to 350°F. Lightly grease and line a nonstick loaf pan. Put the mushrooms, onion, garlic, pepper, stock and wine in a saucepan. Cover and cook for 10 minutes, stirring occasionally.

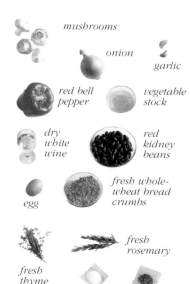

mushrooms
onion
garlic
red bell pepper
vegetable stock
dry white wine
red kidney beans
egg
fresh whole-wheat bread crumbs
fresh thyme
fresh rosemary
salt
black pepper

2 Set aside to cool slightly, then purée the mixture with the kidney beans in a blender or food processor until smooth.

3 Transfer the mixture to a bowl, add the egg, bread crumbs and herbs and mix thoroughly. Season to taste.

4 Spoon into the prepared pan and level the surface. Bake for 45–60 minutes, until lightly set and browned on top. Place on a wire rack and allow the pâté to cool completely in the pan. Once cool, cover and refrigerate for several hours. Turn out of the pan and serve in slices. Garnish with lettuce and tomatoes.

NUTRITIONAL NOTES
PER PORTION:

CALORIES 53 PROTEIN 3.42g
FAT 1.04g SATURATED FAT 0.26g
CARBOHYDRATE 7.65g FIBER 2.33g
ADDED SUGAR 0.00g SODIUM 0.11g

Lima Bean, Watercress and Herb Dip

A refreshing dip that is especially good served with fresh vegetable crudités and breadsticks.

Serves 4–6

INGREDIENTS

1 cup plain cottage cheese
1 can (14 ounces) lima beans, rinsed and drained
1 bunch scallions, chopped
2 ounces watercress, chopped
4 tablespoons reduced-calorie mayonnaise
3 tablespoons chopped fresh mixed herbs
salt and ground black pepper
watercress sprigs, to garnish

lima beans *cottage cheese*

scallions

watercress

mayonnaise

salt

black pepper

fresh mixed herbs

NUTRITIONAL NOTES

PER PORTION:

CALORIES 155 PROTEIN 12.45
FAT 6.98g SATURATED FAT 2.04g
CARBOHYDRATE 11.25g FIBER 3.49g
ADDED SUGAR 0.38g SODIUM 0.63g

1 Put the cottage cheese, lima beans, scallions, watercress, mayonnaise and herbs in a blender or food processor and blend until you have a coarse paste.

2 Add seasoning and spoon the mixture into a dish.

COOK'S TIP

Try using other canned beans such as cannellini beans or chickpeas in place of the lima beans.

3 Cover and chill for several hours before serving.

4 Transfer to a serving dish (or individual dishes), and garnish with watercress sprigs.

Vegetables Provençal

The flavors of the Mediterranean are created in this delicious vegetable dish, ideal for a first course or lunchtime snack, served with fresh, crusty whole-wheat bread.

Serves 6

INGREDIENTS
1 onion, sliced
2 leeks, sliced
2 garlic cloves, crushed
1 each red, green, and yellow bell
  pepper, seeded and sliced
12 ounces zucchini, sliced
3 cups mushrooms, sliced
1 can (14 ounces) chopped
  tomatoes
2 tablespoons ruby port
2 tablespoons tomato paste
1 tablespoon ketchup
1 can (14 ounces) chickpeas
1 cup pitted black olives
3 tablespoons fresh mixed herbs
salt and ground black pepper
chopped fresh mixed herbs,
  to garnish

onion   *leeks*

garlic   *red
           pepper*

*yellow
pepper*   *green
           pepper*

zucchini   *mushrooms*

*chopped
tomatoes*   *ruby
            port*   *tomato
                     paste*

ketchup   *chickpeas*   *pitted black
                           olives*   *fresh mixed
                                      herbs*

1 Put the onion, leeks, garlic, peppers, zucchini and mushrooms in a large saucepan.

2 Add the tomatoes, port, tomato paste and ketchup and mix well.

3 Rinse and drain the chickpeas and add to the pan.

4 Cover, bring to a boil and simmer gently for 20–30 minutes, stirring occasionally, until the vegetables are cooked and tender but not overcooked.

5 Remove the lid and increase the heat slightly for the last 10 minutes of the cooking time to thicken the sauce, if desired.

6 Stir in the olives, herbs and seasoning. Serve hot or cold garnished with chopped mixed herbs.

NUTRITIONAL NOTES
PER PORTION:

CALORIES 155 PROTEIN 8.26g
FAT 4.56g SATURATED FAT 0.67g
CARBOHYDRATE 20.19g FIBER 6.98g
ADDED SUGAR 0.52g SODIUM 0.62g

Warm Chicken Salad with Shallots and Snow Peas

Succulent cooked chicken pieces are combined with vegetables in a light chili dressing.

Serves 6

INGREDIENTS
2 ounces mixed lettuce leaves
2 ounces baby spinach leaves
2 ounces watercress
2 tablespoons chili sauce
2 tablespoons dry sherry
1 tablespoon light soy sauce
1 tablespoon ketchup
2 teaspoons olive oil
8 shallots, finely chopped
1 garlic clove, crushed
12 ounces skinless, boneless
   chicken breast, cut into thin strips
1 red bell pepper, sliced
6 ounces snow peas, trimmed
1 can (14 ounces) baby corn,
   drained and halved
1 cup brown rice
salt and ground black pepper
parsley sprig to garnish

1 Arrange the mixed lettuce leaves, tearing up any large ones, and the spinach leaves on a serving dish. Add the watercress and toss to mix.

2 In a small bowl, mix together the chili sauce, sherry, soy sauce and ketchup and set aside.

mixed lettuce leaves　*spinach*　*watercress*　*chili sauce*　*dry sherry*

light soy sauce　*ketchup*　*olive oil*　*shallots*　*garlic*

chicken breasts　*red bell pepper*　*snow peas*　*baby corn*　*brown rice*

3 Heat the oil in a large nonstick frying pan or wok. Add the shallots and garlic and stir-fry over medium heat for 1 minute.

4 Add the chicken and stir-fry for 3–4 minutes.

NUTRITIONAL NOTES

PER PORTION:

CALORIES 188 PROTEIN 19.22g
FAT 2.81g SATURATED FAT 0.52g
CARBOHYDRATE 21.39g FIBER 3.07g
ADDED SUGAR 0.71g SODIUM 1.07g

COOK'S TIP
Use other lean meat such as turkey breast, beef or pork in place of the chicken.

5 Add the pepper, snow peas, corn and rice and stir-fry for 2–3 minutes.

6 Pour in the chili sauce mixture and stir-fry for 2–3 minutes, until hot and bubbling. Season to taste. Spoon the chicken mixture over the salad leaves, toss together to mix and serve immediately, garnished with fresh parsley.

Pork and Vegetable Stir-fry

A quick and easy stir-fry of pork and vegetables.

Serves 4

INGREDIENTS
1 can (8 ounces) pineapple cubes
1 tablespoon cornstarch
2 tablespoons light soy sauce
1 tablespoon each dry sherry,
  brown sugar and wine vinegar
1 teaspoon five-spice powder
2 teaspoons olive oil
1 red onion, sliced
1 garlic clove, crushed
1 fresh seeded red chili, chopped
1-inch piece fresh ginger
12 ounces lean pork tenderloin,
  cut into thin strips
6 ounces carrots
1 red bell pepper, seeded
  and sliced
6 ounces snow peas, halved
½ cup bean sprouts
1 can (7 ounces) corn kernels
2 tablespoons chopped cilantro
salt
1 tablespoon toasted sesame seeds,
  to garnish

pineapple cubes

light soy sauce

dry sherry

wine vinegar

five-spice powder

olive oil

red onion

garlic

red chili

ginger

red bell pepper

carrots

snow peas

pork tenderloin

corn kernels

cilantro

bean sprouts

1 Drain the pineapple, reserving the juice. In a small bowl, blend the cornstarch with the pineapple juice. Add the soy sauce, sherry, sugar, vinegar and spice, stir to mix and set aside.

2 Heat the oil in a large nonstick frying pan or wok. Add the onion, garlic, chili and ginger and stir-fry for 30 seconds. Add the pork and stir-fry for 2–3 minutes.

NUTRITIONAL NOTES
PER PORTION:

CALORIES 327 PROTEIN 24.95g
FAT 7.90g SATURATED FAT 1.89g
CARBOHYDRATE 40.81g FIBER 4.77g
ADDED SUGAR 5.38g SODIUM 0.73g

3 Cut the carrots into matchstick strips. Add to the wok with the pepper and stir-fry for 2–3 minutes. Add the snow peas, bean sprouts and corn and stir-fry for 1–2 minutes.

4 Pour in the sauce mixture and the reserved pineapple and stir-fry until the sauce thickens. Reduce the heat and stir-fry for another 1–2 minutes. Stir in the cilantro and season to taste. Sprinkle with sesame seeds and serve immediately.

Lamb with Vegetables

Lots of vegetables make this a healthy dish.

Serves 6

INGREDIENTS
juice of 1 lemon
1 tablespoon soy sauce
1 tablespoon dry sherry
1 garlic clove, crushed
2 teaspoons chopped fresh rosemary
6 lean shoulder or loin lamb chops
1 red onion, cut into 8 pieces
1 onion, cut into 8 pieces
1 each red, yellow, and green bell
 pepper, cut into chunks
4 zucchini, thickly sliced
12 ounces button mushrooms
2 tablespoons olive oil
4 plum tomatoes, peeled
1 can (14 ounces) baby corn
4 tablespoons chopped fresh basil
1–2 tablespoons balsamic vinegar
salt and ground black pepper
fresh herbs and basil sprig, to garnish

lemon juice   *soy sauce*   *dry sherry*   *garlic*

fresh rosemary   *loin lamb chops*   *red onion*   *onion*

peppers   *zucchini*   *button mushrooms*

olive oil   *plum tomatoes*   *baby corn*

balsamic vinegar   *basil sprig*

1 In a shallow dish, mix together the lemon juice, soy sauce, sherry, garlic and rosemary. Coat the lamb chops in the marinade. Cover and refrigerate for 2 hours.

2 Preheat the oven to 400°F. Put the onions, peppers, zucchini and mushrooms in a roasting pan, drizzle with the oil and toss the vegetables. Bake for 25 minutes.

NUTRITIONAL NOTES

PER PORTION:

CALORIES 273 PROTEIN 26.95g
FAT 4.22g SATURATED FAT 4.22g
CARBOHYDRATE 13.15g FIBER 4.99g
ADDED SUGAR 0.10g SODIUM 0.91g

3 Quarter the tomatoes and stir in to the roasting pan with the corn. Bake for another 10 minutes, until the vegetables are just tender and browned at the edges. Add the basil, sprinkle with the balsamic vinegar and season to taste, stirring to mix.

4 Preheat the broiler. Place the lamb chops under a medium broiler and broil for 6 minutes on each side until cooked turning over once. While the chops are cooking, brush with remaining marinade to prevent them from drying out. Serve the chops with the cooked vegetables and garnish with fresh chopped herbs and a basil sprig.

Spiced Lamb and Vegetable Couscous

A delicious stew of tender lamb and vegetables served with couscous.

Serves 6

INGREDIENTS

12 ounces lean lamb cutlet, cut into ¾-inch cubes
2 tablespoons whole-wheat flour, seasoned
2 teaspoons sunflower oil
1 onion, chopped
2 garlic cloves, crushed
1 red bell pepper, seeded and diced
1 teaspoon ground coriander
1 teaspoon ground cumin
1 teaspoon ground allspice
½ teaspoon chili powder
1 cup lamb or beef stock
1 can (14 ounces) chopped tomatoes
8 ounces carrots, sliced
6 ounces parsnips, sliced
6 ounces zucchini, sliced
6 ounces small mushrooms, quartered
8 ounces fava beans
¾ cup golden raisins
1 pound quick-cooking couscous
salt and ground black pepper
cilantro, to garnish

1 Toss the lamb in the flour. Heat the oil in a large saucepan and add the lamb, onion, garlic and pepper. Cook for 5 minutes, stirring frequently.

2 Add any remaining flour and the spices and cook for 1 minute, stirring.

3 Gradually add the stock, stirring continuously, then add the tomatoes, carrots and parsnips and mix well.

4 Bring to a boil, stirring, then cover and simmer for 30 minutes, stirring occasionally.

lamb cutlet

whole-wheat flour

sunflower oil

onion

garlic

red bell pepper

ground coriander

ground cumin

ground allspice

chili powder

lamb stock

chopped tomatoes

carrots

parsnips

zucchini

mushrooms

fava beans

golden raisins

couscous

NUTRITIONAL NOTES
PER PORTION:

CALORIES 439 PROTEIN 23.29g
FAT 8.15g SATURATED FAT 2.57g
CARBOHYDRATE 72.98g FIBER 7.34g
ADDED SUGAR 0.00g SODIUM 0.18g

COOK'S TIP

For a tasty alternative, serve the lamb and vegetable stew on a bed of cooked bulgur or brown rice.

5 Add the zucchini, mushrooms, fava beans and golden raisins. Cover, return to a boil and simmer for another 20–30 minutes, stirring occasionally, until the lamb and vegetables are tender. Season to taste.

6 Meanwhile, soak the couscous and steam in a lined colander over a pan of boiling water for about 20 minutes, until cooked, or prepare according to the package instructions. Pile the cooked couscous on a warmed serving platter or individual plates and top with the lamb and vegetable stew. Garnish with cilantro and serve immediately.

Chicken and Bean Risotto

Brown rice, red kidney beans, corn and broccoli all add extra fiber to this risotto.

Serves 4–6

INGREDIENTS
1 onion, chopped
2 garlic cloves, crushed
1 fresh red chili, seeded and
  finely chopped
6 ounces mushrooms, sliced
2 stalks celery, chopped
1 cup long grain brown rice
2 cups chicken stock
⅔ cup dry white wine
8 ounces cooked skinless chicken
  breast, diced
1 can (14 ounces) red kidney
  beans, drained
1 can (7 ounces) corn, drained
⅔ cup golden raisins
6 ounces small broccoli florets
2–3 tablespoons chopped
  mixed fresh herbs
salt and ground black pepper

onion
garlic
red chili
celery
mushrooms
long grain brown rice
chicken stock
dry white wine
chicken breasts
red kidney beans
corn
golden raisins
broccoli
mixed fresh herbs

1 Put the onion, garlic, chili, mushrooms, celery, rice, stock and wine in a saucepan. Cover, bring to a boil and simmer for 25 minutes.

2 Stir in the chicken, kidney beans, corn and raisins. Cook for another 10 minutes, until almost all the liquid has been absorbed.

NUTRITIONAL NOTES
PER PORTION:

CALORIES 563 PROTEIN 31.01g
FAT 5.73g SATURATED FAT 1.31g
CARBOHYDRATE 96.85g FIBER 8.72g
ADDED SUGAR 0.02g SODIUM 0.66g

3 Meanwhile, cook the broccoli in boiling water for 5 minutes, then drain thoroughly.

4 Stir in the broccoli and chopped herbs, season to taste and serve immediately.

COOK'S TIP
Use 1 teaspoon chili powder in place of the fresh chili.

Smoked Bacon and Green Bean Pasta Salad

A tasty pasta salad subtly flavored with smoked bacon and tossed in a light, flavorful dressing.

Serves 4

INGREDIENTS
3 cups whole-wheat rotini
8 ounces green beans
8 slices lean smoked Canadian
  bacon, rind and fat removed
12 ounces cherry tomatoes, halved
2 bunches scallions, chopped
1 can (14 ounces) chickpeas, rinsed
  and drained
6 tablespoons tomato juice
2 tablespoons balsamic vinegar
1 teaspoon ground cumin
1 teaspoon ground coriander
2 tablespoons chopped cilantro
salt and ground black pepper

whole-wheat rotini
green beans
cherry tomatoes
scallions
smoked bacon
chickpeas
tomato juice
balsamic vinegar

ground cumin
ground coriander

cilantro

salt
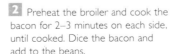
black pepper

1 Cook the pasta in a large saucepan of lightly salted boiling water for 10–12 minutes, until al dente. Meanwhile, trim and halve the green beans and cook them in boiling water for about 5 minutes, until tender. Drain thoroughly and keep warm.

2 Preheat the broiler and cook the bacon for 2–3 minutes on each side, until cooked. Dice the bacon and add to the beans.

3 Put the tomatoes, scallions and chickpeas in a bowl and mix together. In a small bowl, mix together the tomato juice, vinegar, spices, cilantro and seasoning and pour over the tomato mixture.

COOK'S TIP
Always rinse canned beans and peas well before using to remove as much of the brine (saltwater) as possible.

4 Drain the pasta thoroughly and add to the tomato mixture with the beans and bacon. Toss all the ingredients together to mix and serve warm or cold.

NUTRITIONAL NOTES
PER PORTION:

CALORIES 444 PROTEIN 28.43g
FAT 8.67g SATURATED FAT 1.981g
CARBOHYDRATE 68.69g FIBER 13.43g
ADDED SUGAR 0.00g SODIUM 1.26g

Bean and Ham Lasagne

Serve this tasty lasagne with a salad and bread.

Serves 6

INGREDIENTS

2 teaspoons olive oil
3 cups sliced leeks
1 garlic clove, crushed
3 cups mushrooms, sliced
2 zucchini, sliced
12 ounces baby fava beans
2 cups diced lean smoked ham
5 tablespoons chopped fresh
    parsley
2 tablespoons chopped fresh chives
4 tablespoons reduced-fat spread
½ cup whole-wheat flour
2½ cups skim milk
1¼ cups vegetable stock, cooled
6 ounces low-fat cheese
1 teaspoon smooth mustard
8 ounces instant no-boil
    whole-wheat lasagne
½ cup fresh whole-wheat
    bread crumbs
1 tablespoon grated Parmesan
salt and ground black pepper
fresh herb sprigs, to garnish

1 Preheat the oven to 350°F. Heat the oil in a saucepan, add the leeks and garlic and cook, stirring, for 3 minutes. Add the mushrooms and zucchini and cook, stirring, for 5 minutes.

2 Remove the pan from the heat and stir in the fava beans, ham and herbs. Set aside.

olive oil *leeks* *garlic* *mushrooms*

zucchini *baby fava beans* *smoked ham* *fresh parsley* *fresh chives* *reduced-fat spread*

whole-wheat flour *skim milk* *vegetable stock* *mustard* *low-fat cheese*

whole-wheat lasagne *Parmesan cheese* *fresh whole-wheat bread crumbs* *salt* *black pepper*

3 Make the cheese sauce. Put the reduced-fat spread, flour, milk and stock in a saucepan and heat gently, whisking constantly, until the sauce comes to a boil and thickens. Simmer gently for 3 minutes, stirring. Grate the cheese.

4 Remove the pan from the heat, add the mustard and grated cheese and stir until the cheese has melted and is well blended. Season to taste. Reserve ½ cup of cheese sauce and set aside. Mix the remaining sauce with the ham and vegetables.

5 Spoon half the ham mixture over the bottom of a shallow ovenproof dish or baking pan. Cover with half the pasta. Repeat these layers with the remaining ham mixture and pasta, then pour the reserved cheese sauce over the pasta to cover it completely.

6 Mix together the bread crumbs and Parmesan cheese and sprinkle over the lasagne. Bake for 45–60 minutes, until cooked and golden brown on top. Garnish with fresh herb sprigs and serve immediately.

NUTRITIONAL NOTES
PER PORTION:

CALORIES 448 PROTEIN 38.45g
FAT 13.05g SATURATED FAT 5.07g
CARBOHYDRATE 46.16g FIBER 10.86g
ADDED SUGAR 0.02g SODIUM 0.50g

Chicken and Bean Casserole

A delicious combination of chicken, fresh tarragon and mixed beans topped with a layer of tender potatoes, ideal served with broccoli florets and baby carrots for a filling family meal.

Serves 6

INGREDIENTS
2 pounds potatoes
½ cup reduced-fat aged
  Cheddar cheese, finely grated
2½ cups plus 2–3 tablespoons
  skim milk
2 tablespoons chopped fresh chives
2 leeks, washed and sliced
1 onion, sliced
2 tablespoons dry white wine
3 tablespoons reduced-fat spread
¼ cup all-purpose whole-wheat
  flour
1¼ cups chicken stock
12 ounces cooked skinless
  chicken breast, diced
3 cups crimini
  mushrooms, sliced
1 can (11 ounces) red kidney beans
1 can (14 ounces) cannellini beans
1 can (14 ounces) black-eyed peas
2–3 tablespoons chopped
  fresh tarragon
salt and ground black pepper

potatoes

reduced-fat aged Cheddar cheese

skim milk

dry white wine

reduced-fat spread

whole-wheat flour

crimini mushrooms

red kidney beans

fresh chives

leeks

onion

cooked chicken breasts

chicken stock

cannellini beans

black-eyed peas

fresh tarragon

1 Preheat the oven to 400°F. Cut the potatoes into chunks and cook in lightly salted boiling water for 15–20 minutes, until tender. Drain thoroughly and mash. Add the cheese, 2–3 tablespoons milk and chives, season to taste and mix well. Set aside and keep warm.

2 Meanwhile, put the leeks and onion in a saucepan with the wine. Cover and cook gently for 10 minutes, stirring occasionally, until the vegetables are just tender.

3 Put the reduced-fat spread, flour, remaining 2½ cups milk and stock in a saucepan. Heat gently, whisking constantly, until the sauce comes to a boil and thickens. Simmer gently, stirring, for 3 minutes.

4 Remove the pan from the heat and add the leek mixture, chicken and mushrooms and mix well.

5 Rinse and drain all the beans, add to the sauce and stir in the tarragon and seasoning. Heat gently, stirring, until the chicken mixture is piping hot.

COOK'S TIP

Sweet potatoes in place of standard potatoes work just as well in this recipe, and turkey or lean ham can be used in place of the chicken for a change.

6 Transfer mixture to an ovenproof dish and spoon or pipe the potato mixture over the top, covering the chicken mixture completely. Bake for about 30 minutes, until the potato topping is crisp and golden brown. Serve immediately.

NUTRITIONAL NOTES

PER PORTION:

CALORIES 541 PROTEIN 44.98g
FAT 9.36g SATURATED FAT 2.85g
CARBOHYDRATE 72.49g FIBER 16.46g
ADDED SUGAR 0.01g SODIUM 0.62g

Country Chicken Casserole

Succulent chicken quarters in a vegetable sauce
are excellent served with brown rice or pasta.

NUTRITIONAL NOTES

PER PORTION:

CALORIES 360 PROTEIN 37.83g
FAT 9.00g SATURATED FAT 2.11g
CARBOHYDRATE 21.55g FIBER 8.51g
ADDED SUGAR 0.01g SODIUM 0.71g

Serves 4

INGREDIENTS
2 chicken breasts, skinned
2 chicken legs, skinned
salt and ground black pepper
2 tablespoons whole-wheat flour
1 tablespoon sunflower oil
1¼ cups chicken stock
1¼ cups dry white wine
2 tablespoons strained tomatoes
1 tablespoon tomato paste
4 slices smoked Canadian bacon
1 large onion, sliced
1 garlic clove, crushed
1 green bell pepper, seeded
  and sliced
3 cups button mushrooms
8 ounces carrots, sliced
1 bouquet garni
8 ounces frozen Brussels sprouts
1½ cups frozen petit pois
chopped fresh parsley, to garnish

1 Preheat the oven to 350°F. Coat the chicken quarters with seasoned flour.

2 Heat the oil in a large flameproof casserole, add the chicken and cook until browned all over. Remove the chicken using a slotted spoon and keep warm.

3 Add any remaining flour to the pan and cook for 1 minute. Gradually stir in the stock and wine, then add the strained tomatoes and paste.

chicken breasts
and legs

seasoned
whole-wheat
flour

sunflower
oil

chicken
stock

dry
white
wine

strained
tomatoes

tomato
paste

smoked
bacon

onion

garlic

green
pepper

button
mushrooms

carrots

bouquet
garni

Brussels
sprouts

petit pois

4 Bring to a boil, stirring constantly, then add the chicken, bacon, onion, garlic, pepper, mushrooms, carrots and bouquet garni and stir. Cover and bake for 1½ hours, stirring once or twice.

COOK'S TIP
Use fresh Brussels sprouts
and peas if available, and use
red wine in place of white for
a change.

5 Stir in the Brussels sprouts and
petit pois, cover and bake for
another 30 minutes.

6 Remove and discard the bouquet
garni. Add seasoning to the casserole,
garnish with chopped fresh parsley and
serve immediately.

Salmon and Broccoli Pilaf

This quick and easy pilaf is an ideal choice for a tasty suppertime meal.

Serves 4

INGREDIENTS
1 red onion, chopped
1 garlic clove, crushed
4 stalks celery, chopped
1 yellow bell pepper, diced
1 cup brown basmati rice
2½ cups fish stock
1¼ cups dry white wine
1 can (14 ounces) pink salmon, drained and flaked
1 can (14 ounces) red kidney beans, rinsed and drained
12 ounces small broccoli florets
3 tablespoons chopped fresh parsley
1–2 tablespoons light soy sauce
salt and ground black pepper
1 ounce toasted flaked almonds, to garnish

red onion

garlic

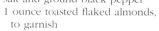
celery

yellow bell pepper

brown basmati rice

fish stock

dry white wine

pink salmon

red kidney beans

broccoli

fresh parsley

1 Put the onion, garlic, celery, pepper, rice, stock and wine in a saucepan and bring to a boil, stirring. Simmer uncovered for 25–30 minutes, until almost all the liquid has been absorbed, stirring occasionally.

2 Stir the salmon and kidney beans into the rice mixture. Cook gently for another 5–10 minutes, until the pilaf is piping hot.

NUTRITIONAL NOTES
PER PORTION:

CALORIES 550 PROTEIN 33.38g
FAT 11.98g SATURATED FAT 2.00g
CARBOHYDRATE 69.55g FIBER 9.51g
ADDED SUGAR 0.71g SODIUM 1.39g

3 Meanwhile, cook the broccoli florets in boiling water for about 5 minutes, until tender. Drain thoroughly and keep warm.

4 Fold the broccoli into the pilaf, then stir in the parsley and soy sauce and season to taste. Garnish with flaked almonds and serve immediately.

Oat-crusted Mackerel

An appetizing way of serving fresh mackerel.
Serve with baked potatoes and cooked snow
peas for a tasty and filling meal.

Serves 4

INGREDIENTS
4 mackerel, each weighing about
  6–8 ounces
juice of 1 lemon
1 cup rolled oats
2 tablespoons chopped fresh
  mixed herbs
salt and ground black pepper
tomato quarters and fresh herb
  sprigs, to garnish

mackerel

*lemon
juice*

rolled oats

*fresh mixed
herbs*

salt

*black
pepper*

1 Remove and discard the heads
from the mackerel, then clean the fish.

2 Sprinkle the inside of each mackerel
with lemon juice and seasoning.

3 Mix together the oats and herbs
and press the oat mixture firmly onto
the outside of each fish.

4 Preheat the broiler. Broil the
fish under fairly hot heat for
6–8 minutes, turning once, until the fish
is cooked, tender and is just beginning
to flake. Garnish with tomato quarters
and fresh herb sprigs.

NUTRITIONAL NOTES
PER PORTION:

CALORIES 480 PROTEIN 36.30g
FAT 30.15g SATURATED FAT 6.18g
CARBOHYDRATE 16.63g FIBER 1.88g
ADDED SUGAR 0.00g SODIUM 0.10g

COOK'S TIP
Sardines or trout can be used in
place of the mackerel in this
recipe and are equally good.

Tuna, Chickpea and Cherry Tomato Salad

A quick and easy salad that makes a satisfying light meal when served with thick slices of whole-wheat bread.

NUTRITIONAL NOTES
PER PORTION:

CALORIES 198 PROTEIN 20.98g
FAT 4.30g SATURATED FAT 0.62g
CARBOHYDRATE 20.70g FIBER 5.88g
ADDED SUGAR 0.00g SODIUM 0.45g

Serves 6

INGREDIENTS
1 teaspoon olive oil
1 garlic clove, crushed
1 teaspoon ground coriander
1 teaspoon garam masala
1 teaspoon chili powder
½ cup tomato juice
2 tablespoons balsamic vinegar
dash of Tabàsco sauce
1½ pounds cherry tomatoes, halved
½ cucumber, sliced
1 bunch radishes, sliced
1 bunch scallions, chopped
2 ounces watercress, chopped
2 cans (14 ounces) chickpeas,
  rinsed and drained
2 cans (14 ounces) tuna in water,
  drained and flaked
1 tablespoon chopped fresh parsley
1 tablespoon chopped fresh chives
salt and ground black pepper

1 Heat the oil in a small saucepan. Add the garlic and spices and cook gently for 1 minute, stirring.

2 Stir in the tomato juice, vinegar and Tabasco sauce, and heat gently until the mixture is boiling. Remove the pan from the heat and set aside to cool slightly.

3 Put the tomatoes and cucumber in a serving bowl.

olive oil   garlic   ground coriander   garam masala   chili powder   tomato juice

balsamic vinegar   Tabasco sauce   cherry tomatoes   cucumber   radishes   scallions

watercress   chickpeas   tuna   fresh parsley   fresh chives

4 Add the radishes, scallions and watercress.

5 Stir in the chickpeas, the tuna and the herbs.

6 Pour the tomato dressing over the salad and toss the ingredients together to mix. Season to taste and serve.

Spicy Seafood and Okra Stew

This spicy combination of seafood and vegetables is good served with herbed brown rice.

Serves 4–6

INGREDIENTS
2 teaspoons olive oil
1 onion, chopped
1 garlic clove, crushed
2 stalks celery, chopped
1 red bell pepper, seeded and diced
1 teaspoon each ground coriander,
  ground cumin and ground ginger
½ teaspoon chili powder
½ teaspoon garam masala
2 tablespoons whole-wheat flour
1¼ cups each fish stock and dry
  white wine
1 can (8 ounces) chopped tomatoes
1 can (8 ounces) okra, trimmed
  and sliced
3 cups mushrooms, sliced
1 pound frozen, cooked, shelled
  seafood, defrosted
1 can (6 ounces) corn kernels
8 ounces long grain brown rice
2–3 tablespoons chopped fresh
  mixed herbs
salt and ground black pepper
fresh parsley sprigs, to garnish

1 Heat the oil in a large saucepan. Add the onion, garlic, celery and pepper and cook for 5 minutes, stirring occasionally.

2 Add the spices and cook for 1 minute, stirring, then add the flour and cook for another 1 minute, stirring.

3 Gradually stir in the stock and wine and add the tomatoes, okra and mushrooms. Bring to a boil, stirring constantly, then cover and simmer for 20 minutes, stirring occasionally.

4 Stir in the seafood and corn and cook for another 10–15 minutes, until piping hot.

olive oil   *onion*   *garlic*   *celery*   *red pepper*   *ground coriander*

ground cumin   *ground ginger*   *chili powder*   *garam masala*   *whole-wheat flour*

fish stock   *dry white wine*   *chopped tomatoes*   *okra*   *mushrooms*

seafood   *corn*   *long grain brown rice*   *fresh mixed herbs*

NUTRITIONAL NOTES
PER PORTION:

CALORIES 541 PROTEIN 34.96g
FAT 7.18g SATURATED FAT 1.42g
CARBOHYDRATE 76.05g FIBER 7.25g
ADDED SUGAR 0.01g SODIUM 1.35g

COOK'S TIP
Use fresh cooked seafood in place of the frozen if it is available.

5 Meanwhile, cook the rice in a large saucepan of lightly salted boiling water for about 35 minutes, until tender.

6 Rinse the rice in fresh boiling water and drain thoroughly, then toss together with the mixed herbs. Season the stew and serve on a bed of herbed rice. Garnish with fresh parsley sprigs.

Salmon, Zucchini and Corn Frittata

A delicious change from an omelet, serve this filling frittata with a mixed tomato and pepper salad and warm whole-wheat rolls.

NUTRITIONAL NOTES
PER PORTION:

CALORIES 336 PROTEIN 25.85g
FAT 12.20g SATURATED FAT 3.57g
CARBOHYDRATE 32.83g FIBER 4.34g
ADDED SUGAR 0.00g SODIUM 0.49g

COOK'S TIP
Use canned tuna or crab in place of the salmon and mushrooms instead of the zucchini.

Serves 4–6

INGREDIENTS
2 teaspoons olive oil
1 onion, chopped
6 ounces zucchini, thinly sliced
8 ounces boiled potatoes (with skins left on), diced
3 eggs, plus 2 egg whites
2 tablespoons skim milk
1 can (7 ounces) pink salmon in water, drained and flaked
1 can (7 ounces) corn kernels, drained
2 teaspoons dried mixed herbs
salt and ground black pepper
½ cup reduced-fat, aged Cheddar cheese, finely grated
chopped fresh mixed herbs and basil leaves, to garnish

olive oil
onion
zucchini
potatoes
eggs
skim milk
pink salmon
corn
dried mixed herbs
salt
black pepper
Cheddar cheese

1 Heat the oil in a large nonstick frying pan. Add the onion and zucchini and cook for 5 minutes, . stirring occasionally.

2 Add the potatoes and cook for 5 minutes, stirring occasionally.

3 Beat the eggs, egg whites and milk together; add the salmon, corn, herbs and seasoning and pour the mixture evenly over the vegetables.

4 Cook over medium heat until the eggs are beginning to set and the frittata is golden brown underneath.

5 Preheat the broiler. Sprinkle the cheese over the frittata and place it under medium heat until the cheese has melted and the top is golden brown.

6 Sprinkle with chopped fresh herbs, garnish with basil leaves and serve immediately, cut into wedges.

Vegetable Paella

A delicious change from the more traditional seafood-based paella, this recipe is full of flavor and nutrients, including fiber.

Serves 6

INGREDIENTS
1 onion, chopped
2 garlic cloves, crushed
8 ounces leeks (trimmed weight), washed and sliced
3 stalks celery, chopped
1 red bell pepper, seeded and sliced
2 zucchini, sliced
6 ounces crimini mushrooms, sliced
1½ cups frozen peas
2 cups long grain brown rice
1 can (14 ounces) cannellini beans, rinsed and drained
3¾ cups vegetable stock
4 tablespoons dry white wine
few saffron strands
2 cups cherry tomatoes, halved
3–4 tablespoons chopped fresh mixed herbs
salt and ground black pepper
lemon wedges and celery leaves, to garnish

onion *garlic* *leeks*
celery
red pepper
zucchini
cannellini beans *vegetable stock* *dry white wine* *crimini mushrooms* *frozen peas* *brown rice*
fresh mixed herbs *salt* *saffron strands* *cherry tomatoes*
black pepper

1 Put the onion, garlic, leeks, celery, pepper, zucchini and mushrooms in a large saucepan and mix together.

2 Add the peas, rice, cannellini beans, stock, wine and saffron.

3 Bring to a boil, stirring, then simmer uncovered for about 35 minutes, stirring occasionally, until almost all the liquid has been absorbed and the rice is tender.

4 Stir in the tomatoes, chopped herbs and seasoning. Serve garnished with lemon wedges and celery leaves.

NUTRITIONAL NOTES
PER PORTION:

CALORIES 416 PROTEIN 13.69g
FAT 3.95g SATURATED FAT 0.86g
CARBOHYDRATE 84.87g FIBER 8.85g
ADDED SUGAR 0.03g SODIUM 0.54g

Vegetable Chili

This alternative to traditional chili con carne is delicious served with brown rice.

Serves 4

INGREDIENTS
2 onions, chopped
1 garlic clove, crushed
3 stalks celery, chopped
1 green bell pepper, seeded and diced
8 ounces mushrooms, sliced
2 zucchini, diced
1 can (14 ounces) red kidney beans, rinsed and drained
1 can (14 ounces) chopped tomatoes
⅔ cup strained tomatoes
2 tablespoons tomato paste
1 tablespoon ketchup
1 teaspoon chili powder, ground cumin and ground coriander
salt and ground black pepper
cilantro sprigs, to garnish
plain yogurt and cayenne pepper, to serve

onions

garlic

celery

mushrooms

green pepper

zucchini

chopped tomatoes

strained tomatoes

red kidney beans

ketchup

chili powder

tomato paste

ground cumin

ground coriander

1 Put the onions, garlic, celery, pepper, mushrooms and zucchini in a large saucepan and mix together.

2 Add the kidney beans, chopped and strained tomatoes, tomato paste and ketchup.

NUTRITIONAL NOTES
PER PORTION:

CALORIES 158 PROTEIN 9.96g
FAT 1.59g SATURATED FAT 0.27g
CARBOHYDRATE 27.55g FIBER 8.58g
ADDED SUGAR 0.57g SODIUM 0.39g

3 Add the spices and seasoning and mix well.

4 Cover, bring to a boil and simmer, stirring occasionally, for 20–30 minutes, until the vegetables are tender. Garnish with cilantro sprigs. Serve with plain yogurt, sprinkled with cayenne pepper.

Cheese, Onion and Mushroom Flan

A tasty, savory flan is ideal served with slices of whole-wheat bread and a mixed green salad for extra fiber, vitamins and minerals.

NUTRITIONAL NOTES
PER PORTION:

CALORIES 295 PROTEIN 12.75g
FAT 15.52g SATURATED FAT 4.10g
CARBOHYDRATE 27.97g FIBER 4.22g
ADDED SUGAR 0.00g SODIUM 0.27g

COOK'S TIP
Make this savory flan in advance and freeze for up to 3 months. Defrost thoroughly and reheat to serve.

Serves 6

INGREDIENTS
1½ cups all-purpose whole-wheat flour
pinch of salt
6 tablespoons polyunsaturated margarine
1 onion, sliced
1 leek, washed and sliced
2¼ cups mushrooms, chopped
2 tablespoons vegetable stock
2 eggs
⅔ cup skim milk
4 ounces frozen corn kernels
2 tablespoons chopped fresh chives
1 tablespoon chopped fresh parsley
¾ cup reduced-fat aged Cheddar cheese, finely grated
salt and ground black pepper
chives, to garnish

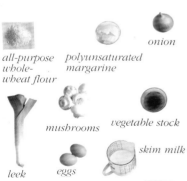

all-purpose whole-wheat flour *polyunsaturated margarine* *onion*

mushrooms *vegetable stock*

leek *eggs* *skim milk*

chives

corn *parsley* *reduced-fat aged Cheddar cheese*

1 Sift the flour and salt into a bowl. Rub the margarine into the flour until the mixture resembles bread crumbs.

2 Mix in enough cold water to form a soft dough. Wrap and chill for 30 minutes.

3 Put the onion, leek, mushrooms and stock in a saucepan. Cover and cook gently for 10 minutes, until the vegetables are just cooked and tender. Drain.

4 Roll the pastry out on a lightly floured surface and use to line an 8-inch round pan or dish. Place on a baking sheet.

5 Spoon the vegetables over the pastry shell. Beat the eggs and milk together, add the corn, herbs, cheese and seasoning and mix well.

6 Pour the egg mixture over the vegetables. Bake for 20 minutes, then reduce the temperature to 350°F, and cook for another 30 minutes, until set and lightly browned. Garnish with chives and serve warm or cold in slices.

Sweet and Sour Mixed Bean Hot Pot

An appetizing mixture of beans and vegetables in a tasty sweet and sour sauce, topped with potato.

Serves 6

INGREDIENTS

1 pound unpeeled potatoes
1 tablespoon olive oil
3 tablespoons reduced-fat spread
¼ cup whole-wheat flour
1¼ cups strained tomatoes
⅔ cup unsweetened apple juice
4 tablespoons each light brown
   sugar, ketchup, dry sherry,
   cider vinegar and light soy sauce
1 can (14 ounces) lima beans
1 can (14 ounces) red kidney beans
1 can (14 ounces) cannellini beans
1 can (14 ounces) chickpeas
6 ounces green beans, chopped
   and blanched
8 ounces shallots, sliced and
   blanched
3 cups mushrooms, sliced
1 tablespoon each chopped fresh
   thyme and marjoram
salt and ground black pepper
fresh herb sprigs, to garnish

1 Preheat the oven to 400°F. Thinly slice the potatoes and parboil them for 4 minutes. Drain thoroughly, toss them in the oil so they are lightly coated all over and set aside.

2 Place the reduced-fat spread, flour, strained tomatoes, apple juice, sugar, ketchup, sherry, vinegar and soy sauce in a saucepan. Heat gently, whisking constantly, until the sauce comes to a boil and thickens. Simmer gently, stirring, for 3 minutes.

3 Rinse and drain the beans and chickpeas and add to the sauce with all the remaining ingredients except the herb garnish. Mix well.

potatoes

olive oil

reduced-fat spread

ketchup

light brown sugar

dry sherry

all-purpose whole-wheat flour

strained tomatoes

unsweetened apple juice

cider vinegar

light soy sauce

lima beans

red kidney beans

cannellini beans

chickpeas

green beans

shallots

mushrooms

fresh thyme

fresh marjoram

4 Spoon the bean mixture into a casserole.

5 Arrange the potato slices over the top, completely covering the bean mixture.

6 Cover the dish with foil and bake for about 1 hour, until the potatoes are cooked and tender. Remove the foil for the last 20 minutes of the cooking time, to lightly brown the potatoes. Serve garnished with fresh herb sprigs.

NUTRITIONAL NOTES
Per portion:

CALORIES 410 PROTEIN 17.36g
FAT 7.43g SATURATED FAT 1.42g
CARBOHYDRATE 70.40g FIBER 12.52g
ADDED SUGAR 15.86g SODIUM 1.54g

Fruity Rice Salad

An appetizing and colorful rice salad combining many different flavors, ideal for a packed lunch.

Serves 4–6

INGREDIENTS

1 cup mixed brown and
  wild rice
1 yellow bell pepper,
  seeded and diced
1 bunch scallions, chopped
3 stalks celery, chopped
1 large beefsteak tomato, chopped
2 green apples, chopped
¾ cup dried apricots, chopped
⅔ cup raisins
2 tablespoons unsweetened
  apple juice
2 tablespoons dry sherry
2 tablespoons light soy sauce
dash of Tabasco sauce
2 tablespoons chopped fresh parsley
1 tablespoon chopped fresh
  rosemary
salt and ground black pepper

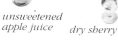
mixed brown
and wild rice

yellow bell
pepper

scallions

celery

beefsteak
tomato

apples

dried
apricots

raisins

unsweetened
apple juice

dry sherry

light soy
sauce

Tabasco
sauce

fresh
parsley

fresh
rosemary

1 Cook the rice in a large saucepan of lightly salted boiling water for about 30 minutes (or according to the instructions on the package), until tender. Rinse the rice under cold running water to cool quickly and drain thoroughly.

2 Place the pepper, scallions, celery, tomato, apples, apricots, raisins and the cooked rice in a serving bowl and mix well.

3 In a small bowl, mix together the apple juice, sherry, soy sauce, Tabasco sauce, herbs and seasoning.

NUTRITIONAL NOTES

PER PORTION:

CALORIES 428 PROTEIN 8.15g
FAT 2.50g SATURATED FAT 0.52g
CARBOHYDRATE 97.15g FIBER 7.17g
ADDED SUGAR 0.31g SODIUM 0.58g

4 Pour the dressing over the rice mixture and toss the ingredients together to mix. Serve immediately, or cover and chill in the fridge before serving.

Bulgur and Fava Bean Salad

This appetizing salad is ideal served with fresh, crusty whole-wheat bread and homemade chutney, and for non-vegetarians it can be served as an accompaniment to grilled lean meat or fish.

Serves 6

INGREDIENTS
2 cups bulgur
8 ounces frozen fava beans
1 cup frozen petit pois
8 ounces cherry tomatoes, halved
1 scallion, chopped
1 red bell pepper, seeded and diced
2 ounces snow peas, chopped
2 ounces watercress
1 tablespoon chopped fresh parsley
1 tablespoon chopped fresh basil
1 tablespoon chopped fresh thyme
salt and ground black pepper
fat-free French dressing

bulgur

*frozen fava
beans*

*frozen
petit
pois*

*cherry
tomatoes*

scallion

*red bell
pepper*

***man**ow peas*

watercress

*fresh
parsley*

fresh basil

*fresh
thyme*

*fat-free
French
dressing*

salt

black pepper

1 Soak and cook the bulgur according to the package instructions. Drain thoroughly and put into a serving bowl.

2 Meanwhile, cook the fava beans and petits pois in boiling water for about 3 minutes, until tender. Drain thoroughly and add to the prepared bulgur.

3 Add the cherry tomatoes, scallion, pepper, snow peas and watercress to the bulgur mixture and mix.

NUTRITIONAL NOTES

PER PORTION:

CALORIES 277 PROTEIN 11.13g
FAT 1.81g SATURATED FAT 0.17g
CARBOHYDRATE 55.34g FIBER 4.88g
ADDED SUGAR 0.00g SODIUM 0.02g

4 Add the herbs, seasoning and French dressing to taste, tossing the ingredients together. Serve immediately or cover and chill in the refrigerator before serving.

COOK'S TIP

Use cooked couscous, brown rice or whole-wheat pasta in place of the bulgur.

Zucchini, Corn and Plum Tomato Whole-wheat Pizza

This tasty whole-wheat pizza can be served hot or cold with a mixed bean salad and fresh crusty bread or baked potatoes. It is also ideal as a snack for the road.

NUTRITIONAL NOTES
PER PORTION:

CALORIES 291 PROTEIN 12.56g
FAT 12.35g SATURATED FAT 3.69g
CARBOHYDRATE 34.54g FIBER 4.93g
ADDED SUGAR 0.00g SODIUM 0.25g

Serves 6

INGREDIENTS
2 cups whole-wheat flour
pinch of salt
2 teaspoons baking powder
¼ cup polyunsaturated margarine
⅔ cup skim milk
2 tablespoons tomato paste
2 teaspoons dried *herbes de Provence*
2 teaspoons olive oil
1 onion, sliced
1 garlic clove, crushed
2 small zucchini, sliced
1½ cups mushrooms, sliced
¾ cup frozen corn kernels
2 plum tomatoes, sliced
½ cup reduced-fat Cheddar cheese, finely grated
½ cup mozzarella cheese, finely grated
salt and ground black pepper
basil sprigs, to garnish

whole-wheat flour

salt

baking powder

dried herbes de Provence

olive oil

onion

tomato paste

garlic

zucchini

mushrooms

plum tomatoes

reduced-fat Cheddar cheese

corn

polyunsaturated margarine *skim milk*

mozzarella cheese

1 Preheat the oven to 425°F. Line a baking sheet with nonstick baking paper. Put the flour, salt and baking powder in a bowl and rub the margarine lightly into the flour until the mixture resembles bread crumbs.

2 Add enough milk to form a soft dough and knead lightly. On a lightly floured surface, roll the dough out to a circle about 10 inches in diameter.

3 Place the dough on the prepared baking sheet and pinch the edges until they are slightly thicker than the center. Spread the tomato paste over the base and sprinkle the herbs on top.

4 Heat the oil in a frying pan, add the onion, garlic, zucchini and mushrooms and cook gently, stirring occasionally, for 10 minutes.

5 Spread the vegetable mixture over the pizza crust and sprinkle with the corn and seasoning. Arrange the tomato slices on top.

6 Mix together the cheeses and sprinkle over the pizza. Bake for 25–30 minutes, until the pizza is cooked and golden brown. Serve hot or cold in slices, garnished with basil sprigs.

COOK'S TIP
This pizza is ideal for freezing in portions or slices. Freeze for up to three months.

Roast Pepper and Wild Mushroom Pasta Salad

A combination of grilled peppers and wild mushrooms makes this pasta salad colorful as well as nutritious.

Serves 6

INGREDIENTS

1 red bell pepper, halved
1 yellow bell pepper, halved
1 green bell pepper, halved
3 cups whole-wheat
  pasta shells or twists
2 tablespooons olive oil
3 tablespooons balsamic vinegar
5 tablespooons tomato juice
2 tablespooons chopped fresh basil
1 tablespooon chopped fresh thyme
2¼ cups shiitake mushrooms,
  sliced
2⅓ cups oyster mushrooms,
  sliced
1 can (14 ounces) black-eyed
  peas, rinsed and drained
⅔ cup golden raisins
2 bunches scallions,
  finely chopped
salt and ground black pepper

red bell
pepper

yellow bell
pepper

green bell
pepper

whole-wheat
pasta shells

olive oil

*balsamic
vinegar*

tomato
juice

fresh basil

*fresh
thyme*

shiitake
mushrooms

oyster
mushrooms

black-eyed
peas

golden
raisins

scallions

1 Preheat the broiler. Put the peppers cut side down on a broiler-pan rack and place under a hot broiler for 10–15 minutes, until the skins are charred. Cover the peppers with a clean, damp dishtowel and set aside to cool.

2 Meanwhile, cook the pasta in lightly salted boiling water for 10–12 minutes, until al dente, then drain thoroughly.

3 Mix together the oil, vinegar, tomato juice, basil and thyme, add to the warm pasta and toss together.

NUTRITIONAL NOTES
PER PORTION:

CALORIES 334 PROTEIN 13.58g
FAT 6.02g SATURATED FAT 0.89g
CARBOHYDRATE 60.74g FIBER 9.37g
ADDED SUGAR 0.00g SODIUM 0.11g

4 Remove and discard the skins from the peppers. Seed and slice the peppers and add to the pasta with the mushrooms, black-eyed peas, raisins, scallions and seasoning. Toss the ingredients to mix and serve immediately, or cover and chill in the refrigerator before serving.

Carrot, Raisin and Apricot Coleslaw

A tasty, high-fiber coleslaw, combining cabbage, carrots and dried fruit in a light yogurt dressing.

Serves 6

INGREDIENTS
3 cups finely shredded white
  cabbage
1½ cups coarsely grated carrots
1 red onion, sliced
3 celery stalks, sliced
1 cup raisins
3 ounces dried apricots, chopped
8 tablespoons reduced-calorie
  mayonnaise
6 tablespoons low-fat plain yogurt
2 tablespoons chopped fresh
  mixed herbs
salt and ground black pepper

white cabbage

carrots

red onion

celery

raisins

dried apricots

reduced-calorie mayonnaise

low-fat plain yogurt

fresh mixed herbs

salt

black pepper

1 Put the cabbage and carrots in a large bowl.

2 Add the onion, celery, raisins and apricots and mix well.

NUTRITIONAL NOTES
PER PORTION:
CALORIES 204 PROTEIN 3.71g
FAT 6.37g SATURATED FAT 0.93g
CARBOHYDRATE 35.04g FIBER 4.25g
ADDED SUGAR 0.50g SODIUM 0.24g

3 In a small bowl, mix together the mayonnaise, yogurt, herbs and seasoning.

COOK'S TIP
Use other dried fruit such as golden raisins and dried pears or peaches in place of the dark raisins and apricots.

4 Add the mayonnaise dressing to the cabbage mixture and toss the ingredients together to mix. Cover and chill for several hours before serving.

Curried New Potato and Green Bean Salad

Tender new potatoes and green beans tossed together in a subtly flavored light dressing make this salad ideal for serving with grilled vegetables and fresh whole-wheat bread.

Serves 6

INGREDIENTS

1½ cups green beans,
  trimmed and halved
1½ pounds cooked baby new
  potatoes
2 bunches scallions, chopped
¾ cup golden raisins
3 ounces dried pears, finely chopped
6 tablespoons reduced-calorie
  mayonnaise
4 tablespoons low-fat plain yogurt
2 tablespoons sheep's milk
  yogurt (if available)
1 tablespoon tomato paste
1 tablespoon curry paste
2 tablespoons chopped fresh chives
salt and ground black pepper

green beans

baby new potatoes

scallions

golden raisins

dried pears

reduced-calorie mayonnaise

low-fat plain yogurt

sheep's milk yogurt

tomato paste

curry paste

chives

salt

black pepper

1 Cook the beans in boiling water for about 5 minutes, until tender. Rinse under cold running water to cool them quickly, drain and set aside.

2 Put the potatoes, beans, scallions, golden raisins and pears in a bowl and mix together.

3 In a small bowl, mix together the mayonnaise, yogurts, tomato paste, curry paste, chives and seasoning.

4 Add the dressing to the potato mixture and toss the ingredients together to mix. Cover and allow to stand for at least 1 hour before serving.

NUTRITIONAL NOTES
PER PORTION:

CALORIES 235 PROTEIN 5.17g
FAT 6.10 SATURATED FAT 1.06g
CARBOHYDRATE 42.62g FIBER 3.87g
ADDED SUGAR 0.83g SODIUM 0.22g

Spicy Bean and Lentil Loaf

An appetizing, meat-free and high-fiber savory loaf, ideal for picnics or a packed lunch.

Serves 12

INGREDIENTS
2 teaspoons olive oil
1 onion, finely chopped
1 garlic clove, crushed
2 stalks celery, finely chopped
1 can (14 ounces) red kidney
  beans, rinsed and drained
1 can (14 ounces) lentils, rinsed
  and drained
1 egg
1 carrot, coarsely grated
½ cup hazelnuts, finely chopped
½ cup reduced-fat aged Cheddar
  cheese, finely grated,
1 cup fresh whole-wheat
  bread crumbs
1 tablespoon tomato paste
1 tablespoon ketchup
1 teaspoon each ground cumin,
  ground coriander and
  chili powder
salt and ground black pepper

olive oil

onion

garlic

celery

red kidney beans

lentils

egg

carrot

hazelnuts

reduced-fat aged Cheddar cheese

fresh whole-wheat bread crumbs

tomato paste

ketchup

ground coriander

ground cumin

chili powder

1 Preheat the oven to 350°F. Lightly grease a 2-pound loaf pan. Heat the oil in a saucepan, add the onion, garlic and celery and cook gently for 5 minutes, stirring occasionally. Remove the pan from the heat and cool slightly.

2 Rinse and drain the beans and lentils. Put in a blender or food processor with the onion mixture and egg, and process until smooth.

3 Transfer the mixture to a bowl, add all the remaining ingredients and mix well. Season to taste.

4 Spoon the mixture into the prepared pan and level the surface. Bake for about 1 hour, then remove from the pan and serve hot or cold in slices.

NUTRITIONAL NOTES
PER PORTION:

CALORIES 119 PROTEIN 7.22g
FAT 4.85g SATURATED FAT 0.88g
CARBOHYDRATE 12.57g FIBER 3.31g
ADDED SUGAR 0.19g SODIUM 0.17g

Vegetable and Macaroni Casserole

A tasty change from macaroni and cheese, this
is delicious served with steamed fresh vegetables.

Serves 6

INGREDIENTS
2¼ cups whole-wheat macaroni
2 cups sliced leeks
3 tablespoons vegetable stock
8 ounces broccoli florets
4 tablespoons reduced-fat spread
½ cup all-purpose whole-wheat
  flour
3¾ cups skim milk
1¼ cups grated reduced-fat
  aged Cheddar cheese
1 teaspoon prepared
  English mustard
1 can (11 ounces) corn kernels
salt and ground black pepper
½ cup fresh whole-wheat
  bread crumbs
2 tablespoons chopped fresh
  parsley
2 tomatoes, cut into eighths

*whole-wheat
macaroni*

leeks

*vegetable
stock*

broccoli

*reduced-
fat spread*

*all-purpose
whole-wheat
flour*

skim milk

*reduced-fat
aged
Cheddar
cheese*

*English
mustard*

corn

*fresh
whole-
wheat bread
crumbs*

fresh parsley

tomatoes

1 Preheat the oven to 400°F. Cook
the macaroni in lightly salted boiling
water for about 10 minutes, until just
tender, then drain and keep warm.

2 Cook the leeks in the stock for
about 10 minutes, until tender, then
strain and set aside. Blanch the broccoli
for 2 minutes, drain and set aside.

3 Put the reduced-fat spread, flour
and milk in a saucepan. Heat gently,
whisking constantly, until the sauce
comes to a boil and thickens. Simmer
gently for 3 minutes, stirring.

4 Remove the pan from the heat, add
1 cup cheese and stir until melted and
well blended.

5 Add the macaroni, broccoli,
mustard, corn and seasoning and mix
well. Transfer the mixture to an ovenproof dish.

6 Mix the remaining cheese, bread
crumbs and parsley together and
sprinkle over the top. Arrange the
tomatoes on top and then bake for
30–40 minutes, until golden brown
and bubbling.

NUTRITIONAL NOTES
PER PORTION:

CALORIES 376 PROTEIN 23.30g
FAT 9.68g SATURATED FAT 3.82g
CARBOHYDRATE 52.34g FIBER 7.12g
ADDED SUGAR 0.01g SODIUM 0.53g

Pineapple and Peach Upside Down Cake

A tasty combination of pineapple and peaches, this old favorite is delicious served with low-fat custard or ice cream.

COOK'S TIP
Other combinations of canned and dried fruit such as apricots and pears, or peaches and figs, work just as well.

Serves 6

INGREDIENTS
5 tablespoons light corn syrup
1 can (8 ounces) pineapple cubes
  in fruit juice
¾ cup dried peaches, chopped
¾ cup superfine sugar
8 tablespoons reduced-fat spread
1½ cups self-rising
  whole-wheat flour
1 teaspoon baking powder
2 eggs

corn syrup

pineapple cubes in fruit juice

dried peaches

superfine sugar

reduced-fat spread

self-rising whole-wheat flour

baking powder

eggs

NUTRITIONAL NOTES
PER PORTION:

CALORIES 410 PROTEIN 8.36g
FAT 10.69g SATURATED FAT 2.82g
CARBOHYDRATE 74.73g FIBER 4.94g
ADDED SUGAR 37.51g SODIUM 0.21g

1 Preheat the oven to 350°F. Lightly grease a 7-inch, loose-bottomed round cake pan and line the base with nonstick waxed paper.

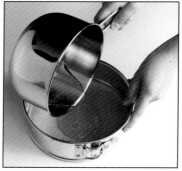

2 Heat the corn syrup gently in a saucepan and pour over the bottom of the pan.

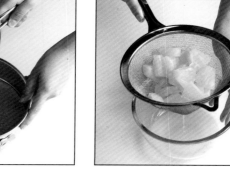

3 Strain the pineapple, reserving 3 tablespoons of the juice.

4 Mix together the pineapple and peaches and sprinkle them over the syrup layer.

5 Put the sugar, reduced-fat spread, flour, baking powder, eggs and reserved pineapple juice in a bowl and beat together until smooth.

6 Spread the cake mixture evenly over the fruit and level the surface. Bake for about 45 minutes, until risen and golden brown. Turn out carefully onto a serving plate and serve hot or cold in slices.

Peach and Raspberry Crisp

A quick and easy tasty dessert, this crisp is good served hot or cold on its own or with low-fat custard.

Serves 4

INGREDIENTS
⅔ cup all-purpose
   whole-wheat flour
¼ cup medium rolled oats
6 tablespoons reduced-fat spread
¼ cup light brown sugar
½ teaspoon ground cinnamon
1 can (14 ounces) peach slices in
   fruit juice
1¼ cups raspberries
2 tablespoons honey

all-purpose whole-wheat flour

rolled oats

reduced-fat spread

light brown sugar

ground cinnamon

peach slices in fruit juice

raspberries

honey

1 Preheat the oven to 350°F. Put the flour and oats in a bowl and mix together.

2 Rub in the reduced-fat spread until the mixture resembles bread crumbs, then stir in the sugar and cinnamon.

3 Drain the peach slices and reserve the juice.

4 Coarsely chop the peaches and put them in an ovenproof dish, then sprinkle the raspberries on top.

5 Mix together the reserved peach juice and honey, pour over the fruit and stir.

6 Spoon the crumb mixture over th fruit, pressing it down lightly. Bake fo about 45 minutes, until golden brov on top. Serve hot or cold.

NUTRITIONAL NOTES
PER PORTION:

CALORIES 334 PROTEIN 7.02g
FAT 9.9g SATURATED FAT 2.51g
CARBOHYDRATE 58.57g FIBER 5.22g
ADDED SUGAR 12.66g SODIUM 0.14g

COOK'S TIP
Use other combinations of fruit, such as apples and blueberries, for a tasty change.

Fruit and Spiced Bread Pudding

An easy-to-make fruit dessert with a hint of spice, which is delicious served either hot or cold.

Serves 4

INGREDIENTS
6 medium slices whole-wheat bread
2 ounces reduced-sugar jam
¼ cup golden raisins
¼ cup dried apricots, chopped
¼ cup light brown sugar
1 teaspoon pumpkin pie spice
2 eggs
2½ cups skim milk
finely grated rind of 1 lemon

whole-wheat bread slices

reduced-sugar jam

golden raisins

dried apricots

light brown sugar

pumpkin pie spice

eggs

skim milk

lemon

NUTRITIONAL NOTES
PER PORTION:

CALORIES 305 PROTEIN 13.77g
FAT 4.51g SATURATED FAT 1.27g
CARBOHYDRATE 56.38g FIBER 3.75g
ADDED SUGAR 13.47g SODIUM 0.38g

1 Preheat the oven to 325°F. Remove and discard the crusts from the bread. Spread the bread slices with jam and cut into small triangles. Place half the bread triangles in a lightly greased oven-proof dish.

2 Mix together the raisins, apricots, sugar and spice and sprinkle half the fruit mixture over the bread in the dish.

3 Top with the remaining bread triangles and then sprinkle the remaining fruit mixture on top.

4 Beat the eggs, milk and lemon rind together and pour over the bread. Set aside for about 30 minutes, to allow the bread to absorb some of the liquid. Bake for 45–60 minutes, until lightly set and golden brown. Serve hot or cold.

Apricot and Banana Compote

This compote is delicious served on its own or with low-fat custard or ice cream. Served for breakfast, it makes a tasty start to the day.

Serves 4

INGREDIENTS
1 cup dried apricots
1¼ cups unsweetened orange juice
⅔ cup unsweetened apple juice
1 teaspoon ground ginger
3 medium bananas, sliced
¼ cup toasted flaked almonds

dried apricots

unsweetened orange juice

unsweetened apple juice

ground ginger

bananas

toasted flaked almonds

1 Put the apricots in a saucepan with the fruit juices and ginger and stir. Cover, bring to a boil and simmer gently for 10 minutes, stirring occasionally.

2 Set aside to cool, leaving the lid on. Once cool, stir in the sliced bananas.

3 Spoon the fruit and juices into a serving dish.

4 Serve immediately, or cover and chill for several hours before serving. Sprinkle with flaked almonds just before serving.

NUTRITIONAL NOTES
PER PORTION:

CALORIES 241 PROTEIN 4.92g
FAT 4.18g SATURATED FAT 0.37g
CARBOHYDRATE 48.98g FIBER 4.91g
ADDED SUGAR 0.00g SODIUM 0.02g

COOK'S TIP
Use other combinations of dried and fresh fruit such as prunes or figs and apples or peaches.

Tropical Fruit Filo Clusters

These fruity filo clusters are ideal for a family treat or a dinner party dessert. They are delicious served either hot or cold, on their own or with reduced-fat cream.

NUTRITIONAL NOTES
PER PORTION:

CALORIES 197 PROTEIN 3.09g
FAT 3.58g SATURATED FAT 0.44g
CARBOHYDRATE 40.21g FIBER 2.31g
ADDED SUGAR 9.96g SODIUM 0.16g

Makes 8

INGREDIENTS
1 banana, sliced
1 small mango, peeled, pitted
  and diced
lemon juice, to sprinkle
1 small cooking apple,
  coarsely grated
6 fresh or dried dates, pitted
  and chopped
2 ounces dried pineapple, chopped
¼ cup golden raisins
¼ cup light brown sugar
1 teaspoon ground mixed spice
8 sheets filo pastry
2 tablespoons sunflower oil
confectioners' sugar, to serve

1 Preheat the oven to 400°F. Line a baking sheet with waxed paper. Toss the banana and mango with lemon juice to prevent discoloration.

2 Add the apple, dates, pineapple, raisins, sugar and spice and mix well.

3 To make each fruit cluster, cut each sheet of filo pastry in half crosswise to make 2 squares/rectangles (16 squares in total). Lightly brush two squares of pastry with oil and place one on top of the other at a 45° angle.

mango   *banana*   *lemon juice*

cooking apple   *dried dates*   *dried pineapple*

golden raisins   *light brown sugar*   *ground mixed spice*

sunflower oil

filo pastry

4 Spoon some fruit filling into the center, gather the pastry up over the filling and secure with string. Place the cluster on the prepared baking sheet and lightly brush all over with oil.

5 Repeat with the remaining pastry squares and filling to make a total of 8 fruit clusters. Bake for 25–30 minutes, until golden brown and crisp.

6 Carefully snip and remove the string from each cluster and serve hot or cold, dusted with sifted confectioners' sugar.

Winter Fruit Salad

A colorful, refreshing and nutritious fruit salad, which is ideal served with reduced-fat plain yogurt or cream.

Serves 6

INGREDIENTS
1 can (8 ounces) pineapple
  cubes in fruit juice
scant cup freshly
  squeezed orange juice
scant cup unsweetened apple juice
2 tablespoons orange or
  apple liqueur
2 tablespoons honey (optional)
2 oranges, peeled
2 green-skinned apples, chopped
2 pears, chopped
4 plums, pitted and chopped
12 fresh dates, pitted and chopped
½ cup dried apricots
fresh mint sprigs, to garnish

pineapple cubes in fruit juice   *freshly squeezed orange juice*

unsweetened apple juice   *orange or apple liqueur*   *honey*

oranges   *green-skinned apples*   *pears*

plums   *fresh dates*   *dried apricots*

1 Drain the pineapple, reserving the juice. Put the pineapple juice, orange juice, apple juice, liqueur and honey, if using, in a large serving bowl and stir.

2 Segment the oranges, catching any juice in the bowl, and put the orange segments and pineapple in the fruit juice mixture.

NUTRITIONAL NOTES
PER PORTION:

CALORIES 227 PROTEIN 2.85g
FAT 0.37g SATURATED FAT 0.00g
CARBOHYDRATE 53.68g FIBER 5.34g
ADDED SUGAR 1.33g SODIUM 0.01g

3 Add the apples and pears to the bowl.

COOK'S TIP
Use other unsweetened fruit juices such as pink grapefruit and pineapple juice in place of the orange and apple juice.

4 Stir in the plums, dates and apricots, cover and chill for several hours. Garnish with fresh mint sprigs to serve.

Whole-wheat Bread and Banana Yogurt Ice

Serve this tempting yogurt ice with some fresh fruit, such as strawberries, or with wafer cookies, for a light dessert.

Serves 6

INGREDIENTS

2 cups fresh whole-wheat
  bread crumbs
¼ cup light brown sugar
1¼ cups low-fat cold custard
5 ounces low-fat ricotta cheese
  or low-fat cream cheese
5 ounces plain yogurt
4 bananas, mashed
juice of 1 lemon
¼ cup confectioners' sugar, sifted
¼ cup raisins, chopped
pared lemon rind, to garnish

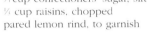
*fresh whole-
wheat bread
crumbs*

*light brown
sugar*

*low-fat cold
custard*

*low-fat
ricotta
cheese*

*plain
yogurt*

bananas

lemon

sugar

raisins

NUTRITIONAL NOTES

PER PORTION:

CALORIES 227 PROTEIN 7.55g
FAT 5.51g SATURATED FAT 2.99g
CARBOHYDRATE 52.27g FIBER 2.01g
ADDED SUGAR 12.77g SODIUM 0.17g

1 Preheat the oven to 400°F. Mix together the bread crumbs and brown sugar and spread the mixture out on a nonstick baking sheet. Bake for about 10 minutes, stirring occasionally, until crisp. Set aside to cool, then break the mixture up into crumbs.

2 Meanwhile, put the custard, ricotta cheese and yogurt in a bowl and mix. Mash the bananas with the lemon juice and add to the custard mixture, mixing well. Fold in the confectioners' sugar.

3 Pour the mixture into a shallow plastic freezer-proof container and freeze for about 3 hours, or until mushy in consistency. Spoon into a chilled bowl and quickly mash with a fork to break down the ice crystals.

4 Add the bread crumb mixture and raisins and mix well. Return to the container, cover and freeze until firm. Soften in the refrigerator for 30 minutes before serving. Garnish with lemon rind.

Pear and Raisin Bran Muffins

These tasty muffins are best eaten freshly baked and served warm or cold, on their own or spread with a little low-fat spread, reduced-sugar jam or honey.

NUTRITIONAL NOTES
PER PORTION:

CALORIES 108 PROTEIN 3.40g
FAT 2.68g SATURATED FAT 0.70g
CARBOHYDRATE 18.84g FIBER 2.64g
ADDED SUGAR 4.37g SODIUM 0.15g

Makes 12

INGREDIENTS
⅔ cup all-purpose whole-wheat flour, sifted
½ cup all-purpose white flour, sifted
3 cups bran
1 tablespoon baking powder, sifted
pinch of salt
¼ cup reduced-fat spread
¼ cup light brown sugar
1 egg
scant cup skim milk
½ cup dried pears, chopped
¼ cup golden raisins

all-purpose whole-wheat flour   *all-purpose white flour*   *bran*

baking powder   *salt*   *reduced-fat spread*

egg

light brown sugar   *skim milk*

dried pears   *golden raisins*

1 Preheat the oven to 400°F. Lightly grease 12 muffin or deep-cup popover pans or line them with paper baking cups. Mix together the flours, bran, baking powder and salt in a bowl.

2 Gently heat the reduced-fat spread in a saucepan until melted.

3 Mix together the melted fat, sugar, egg and milk and pour over the dry ingredients.

4 Gently fold the ingredients together, only enough to combine. The mixture should look quite lumpy, as over-mixing will result in heavy muffins.

5 Fold in the pears and raisins.

COOK'S TIP
For a quick and easy way to chop dried fruit, snip with kitchen scissors.

6 Spoon the mixture into the prepared muffin or popover pans. Bake for 15–20 minutes, until risen and golden brown. Turn out onto a wire rack to cool.

Banana Bran Loaf

A tempting and filling afternoon treat, this loaf is delicious served in slices on its own or spread with a little low-fat spread.

Serves 12

INGREDIENTS
8 tablespoons reduced-fat spread
½ cup light brown sugar
3 eggs, beaten
1½ cups self-rising whole-wheat flour, sifted
3 cups bran
1 teaspoon baking powder, sifted
pinch of salt
1–2 teaspoons ground ginger
3 medium bananas, mashed
1 cup raisins

reduced-fat spread

light brown sugar

eggs

self-rising whole-wheat flour

bran

baking powder

salt

ground ginger

bananas

raisins

NUTRITIONAL NOTES
PER PORTION:

CALORIES 211 PROTEIN 5.42g
FAT 6.11g SATURATED FAT 1.63g
CARBOHYDRATE 36.30g FIBER 3.40g
ADDED SUGAR 9.71g SODIUM 0.09g

1 Preheat the oven to 350°F. Lightly grease a 2-pound loaf pan and line the bottom with waxed paper.

2 Put the reduced-fat spread, sugar, eggs, flour, bran, baking powder, salt and ginger in a bowl and beat together, using a wooden spoon or electric mixer, until thoroughly mixed.

3 Add the mashed bananas to the cake mixture and beat until well mixed.

4 Fold in the raisins.

5 Spoon the mixture into the prepared pan and level the surface.

6 Bake for about 1¼ hours, until risen, golden brown and firm to the touch. Cool in the pan for a few minutes, then turn out onto a wire rack to cool completely. Serve warm or cold in slices.

COOK'S TIP
Use other dried fruit such as chopped dried apricots, prunes or figs in place of the raisins.

Carrot and Coconut Cake

A satisfying cake made with a delicious combination of flavors.

Serves 10

INGREDIENTS
8 tablespoons reduced-fat spread
½ cup superfine sugar
2 eggs
1½ cups self-rising whole-wheat
   flour, sifted
3 cups bran
1 tablespoon baking powder, sifted
6 tablespoons skim milk, plus
   more if needed
1¾ cups carrots, coarsely grated
4 ounces diced coconut
¼ cup golden raisins
finely grated rind of 1 orange
1–2 tablespoons light brown
   granulated sugar, for sprinkling

reduced-fat spread

superfine sugar

eggs

self-rising whole-wheat flour

bran

baking powder

carrots

skim milk

diced coconut

golden raisins

orange

light brown granulated sugar

1 Preheat the oven to 350°F. Lightly grease a deep 7-inch round cake pan and line with waxed paper. Put the reduced-fat spread, sugar, eggs, flour, bran, baking powder and milk in a bowl and beat together until thoroughly mixed.

2 Fold in the carrots, coconut, raisins and orange rind. Add milk until mixture is soft enough to drop from a spoon.

NUTRITIONAL NOTES
PER PORTION:

CALORIES 280 PROTEIN 6.25g
FAT 13.78g SATURATED FAT 7.91g
CARBOHYDRATE 35.17g FIBER 5.61g
ADDED SUGAR 16.13g SODIUM 0.11g

3 Spoon the mixture into the prepared pan and level the surface.

4 Sprinkle the top with granulated sugar and bake for about 1 hour, until risen, golden brown and firm to the touch. Cool in the pan for a few minutes, then turn out onto a wire rack to cool completely. Serve in slices.

Farmhouse Apple and Raisin Cake

A slice of this tasty, moist fruitcake makes an ideal afternoon treat.

Serves 12

INGREDIENTS
¾ cup half-fat spread
¾ cup soft light brown sugar
3 eggs
2 cups self-rising whole-wheat
   flour, sifted
1 cup self-rising white
   flour, sifted
1 teaspoon baking powder, sifted
2 teaspoons pumpkin pie spice
12 ounces cooking apples, peeled,
   cored and diced
1 cup golden raisins
5 tablespoons skim milk
2 tablespoons raw sugar

reduced-fat spread

light brown sugar

eggs

self-rising whole-wheat flour

self-rising white flour

baking powder

pumpkin pie spice

cooking apples

golden raisins

skim milk

raw sugar

1 Preheat the oven to 325°F. Lightly grease a deep 8-inch round loose-bottomed cake pan and line with waxed paper. Put the reduced-fat spread, brown sugar, eggs, flours, baking powder and spice in a bowl and beat together until thoroughly mixed.

2 Fold in the apples, raisins and sufficient milk so that mixture is soft enough to drop from a spoon.

3 Spoon the mixture into the prepared pan and level the surface.

NUTRITIONAL NOTES
PER PORTION:

CALORIES 278 PROTEIN 6.56g
FAT 8.08g SATURATED FAT 2.16g
CARBOHYDRATE 48.55g FIBER 2.60g
ADDED SUGAR 16.95g SODIUM 0.16g

4 Sprinkle the top with raw sugar. Bake for about 1½ hours, until risen, golden brown and firm to the touch. Cool in the pan for a few minutes, then turn out onto a wire rack to cool completely. Serve in slices.

Cheese and Pineapple Whole-wheat Scones

These cheese and pineapple scones are delicious eaten freshly baked, warm or cold, with a little low-fat spread or reduced-sugar jam.

NUTRITIONAL NOTES
PER PORTION:

CALORIES 99 PROTEIN 4.22g
FAT 3.62g SATURATED FAT 1.05g
CARBOHYDRATE 13.28g FIBER 1.74g
ADDED SUGAR 1.33g SODIUM 0.06g

Makes 14–16

INGREDIENTS
2 cups self-rising whole-wheat flour, sifted
1 teaspoon baking powder, sifted
pinch of salt
3 tablespoons polyunsaturated margarine
1 teaspoon mustard powder
¾ cup reduced-fat aged Cheddar cheese, finely grated
¼ cup dried pineapple, finely chopped
⅔ cup skim milk

self-rising whole-wheat flour

baking powder

salt

mustard powder

polyunsaturated margarine

reduced-fat aged Cheddar cheese

dried pineapple

skim milk

1 Preheat the oven to 425°F. Line a baking sheet with waxed paper. Sift the whole-wheat flour, baking powder and salt into a bowl.

2 Rub in the margarine until the mixture resembles bread crumbs.

3 Fold in the mustard powder, cheese, pineapple and enough milk to make a fairly soft dough.

4 Turn the dough out onto a lightly floured surface and knead lightly. Lightly roll out to ¾ inch thickness.

5 Using a 2-inch plain cutter, stamp out rounds and place them on the prepared baking sheet.

6 Brush the tops with milk and bake for about 10 minutes, until risen and golden brown. Transfer to a wire rack to cool and serve warm or cold.

COOK'S TIP

For economy, grate the cheese finely so it will go further and you will use less.

Date and Orange Slices

These tempting, wholesome slices make a tasty treat.

Makes 16

INGREDIENTS
2 cups pitted dried
  dates, finely chopped
scant cup freshly
  squeezed orange juice
finely grated rind of 1 orange
1 cup all-purpose
  whole-wheat flour
1¾ cups rolled oats
½ cup fine oatmeal
pinch of salt
¾ cup reduced-fat spread
¼ cup light brown sugar
2 teaspoons ground cinnamon

dried dates

freshly squeezed orange juice

orange

all-purpose whole-wheat flour

fine oatmeal

rolled oats

salt

reduced-fat spread

light brown sugar

ground cinnamon

1 Preheat the oven to 375°F. Put the dates in a saucepan with the orange juice. Cover, bring to a boil and simmer for 5 minutes, stirring occasionally.

2 Stir in the orange rind and set aside to cool completely.

3 Lightly grease a 7 x 11-inch nonstick cake pan. Put the flour, oats, oatmeal and salt in a bowl and mix together. Lightly rub in the reduced-fat spread.

4 Stir in the sugar and cinnamon. Press half the oat mixture over the bottom of the prepared pan.

5 Spread the date mixture on top and sprinkle the remaining oat mixture evenly over the dates to cover them completely. Press down lightly. Bake for about 30 minutes, until golden brown.

6 Let cool slightly in the pan and mark into 16 bars, using a sharp knife. When firm, remove the slices from the pan and cool completely on a wire rack. Break into bars to serve.

NUTRITIONAL NOTES
PER PORTION:

CALORIES 197 PROTEIN 4.02g
FAT 5.76g SATURATED FAT 1.48g
CARBOHYDRATE 34.06g FIBER 1.76g
ADDED SUGAR 5.25g SODIUM 0.08g

COOK'S TIP
Try using dried apricots or prunes in place of the dates.

Lemon and Raisin Rock Cakes

These lightly spiced, fruit-filled rock buns make an ideal snack or treat.

Makes 16

INGREDIENTS
2 cups self-rising whole-wheat flour
pinch of salt
8 tablespoons reduced-fat spread
¾ cup golden granulated
  or raw sugar
1 teaspoon pumpkin pie spice
finely grated rind of 1 lemon
¾ cup raisins
1 egg, beaten
skim milk, to mix
pared lemon rind, to garnish

self-rising
whole-wheat
flour

salt

reduced-
fat spread

golden
granulated
sugar

pumpkin
pie spice

lemon

raisins

egg

skim milk

NUTRITIONAL NOTES
PER PORTION:

CALORIES 126 PROTEIN 2.90g
FAT 3.64g SATURATED FAT 0.96g
CARBOHYDRATE 21.69g FIBER 1.41g
ADDED SUGAR 7.55g SODIUM 0.06g

1 Preheat the oven to 400°F. Line two baking sheets with waxed paper. Put the whole-wheat flour and salt in a bowl and lightly rub in the reduced-fat spread until the mixture resembles bread crumbs.

2 Mix in the sugar, spice, lemon rind and raisins.

COOK'S TIP
Golden raisins or chopped dried peaches can be used instead of dark raisins, and orange rind instead of lemon rind.

3 Stir in the egg and enough milk to make a stiff, crumbly mixture.

4 Using two spoons, put rough heaps of the mixture on the prepared baking sheets. Bake for 15–20 minutes, until lightly browned and firm to the touch. Transfer to a wire rack to cool. Garnish with lemon rind.

Prune and Nut Loaf

This tasty and filling sweet bread can be served in slices on its own with a little low-fat spread.

Serves 12

INGREDIENTS

1½ cups pitted dried prunes, chopped
¾ cup light brown sugar
1¼ cups cold brewed tea
1 egg, beaten
½ cup hazelnuts, chopped
½ cup walnuts, chopped
2 cups self-rising whole-wheat flour
3 cups bran

dried prunes *light brown sugar*

egg *hazelnuts*

brewed tea

walnuts *self-rising whole-wheat flour*

bran

NUTRITIONAL NOTES

PER PORTION:

CALORIES 223 PROTEIN 5.53g
FAT 6.77g SATURATED FAT 0.67g
CARBOHYDRATE 38.17g FIBER 5.28g
ADDED SUGAR 14.77g SODIUM 0.02g

1 Put the prunes, sugar and tea in a bowl and mix together. Cover and allow to stand for about 4 hours, until most of the tea has been absorbed by the fruit.

2 Preheat the oven to 350°F. Lightly grease a 2-pound loaf pan. Add the egg, nuts, flour and bran to the prune mixture and mix thoroughly.

3 Turn the mixture into the prepared pan and level the surface.

4 Bake for about 1¼ hours and insert a skewer to check that the sweet bread is thoroughly cooked. Cool in the pan for a few minutes, then turn out onto a wire rack to cool completely. Serve in slices.

Cheese and Herb Whole-wheat Soda Bread

Full of flavor, this delicious bread, which is best served freshly baked, warm or cold, can be eaten with a little low-fat spread.

NUTRITIONAL NOTES

PER PORTION:

CALORIES 251 PROTEIN 13.46g
FAT 4.84g SATURATED FAT 1.87g
CARBOHYDRATE 40.94g FIBER 5.18g
ADDED SUGAR 0.00g SODIUM 0.25g

Serves 8

INGREDIENTS

3 cups all-purpose
  whole-wheat flour
1 cup fine oatmeal (see
  Cook's Tip)
2 teaspoons baking soda
2 teaspoons cream of tartar
½ teaspoon salt
1 cup reduced-fat aged Cheddar
  cheese, finely grated
3–4 tablespoons chopped fresh
  mixed herbs
½ teaspoon mustard powder
1¼ cups buttermilk
water, to mix
2 tablespoons skim milk
1 tablespoon rolled oats

all-purpose whole-wheat flour

fine oatmeal

baking soda

cream of tartar

salt

reduced-fat aged Cheddar cheese

fresh mixed herbs

mustard powder

buttermilk

skim milk

rolled oats

1 Preheat the oven to 400°F. Put the flour, fine oatmeal, baking soda, cream of tartar, salt, cheese, herbs and mustard powder in a bowl and mix together.

2 Stir in the buttermilk and enough water to make a soft dough.

3 Lightly knead the dough, then shape into an 8-inch round.

4 Place the round on a lightly greased baking sheet, brush the top with milk and sprinkle with rolled oats.

5 Mark the top into 8 even wedges. Bake for 30–40 minutes, until well risen, firm to the touch and golden brown.

6 Cool on a wire rack. Break into wedges to serve.

COOK'S TIP

To make fine oatmeal, put one cup rolled oats in a blender or food processor and process until fine.

Fruit-filled Muesli Bars

These muesli bars make an appetizing treat
for a snack on the road.

Makes 10–12

INGREDIENTS
8 tablespoons reduced-fat spread
¼ cup light brown sugar
3 tablespoons light corn syrup
1¼ cups no-added-sugar
  Swiss-style muesli or granola
½ cup rolled oats
1 teaspoon pumpkin pie spice
⅓ cup golden raisins
¼ cup dried pears, chopped

reduced-fat spread

light brown sugar

light corn syrup

no-added-sugar Swiss-style muesli

rolled oats

pumpkin pie spice

golden raisins

dried pears

1 Preheat the oven to 350°F. Lightly grease a 7 inch square cake pan.

2 Put the reduced-fat spread, sugar and syrup in a saucepan and gently heat, stirring, until melted and blended.

3 Remove the pan from the heat, add the muesli, oats, spice, golden raisins and pears and mix well.

4 Transfer the mixture to the prepared pan and level the surface, pressing down.

5 Bake for 20–30 minutes, until golden brown. Cool slightly in the pan, then mark into bars using a sharp knife.

6 When firm, remove the muesli bars from the pan and cool on a wire rack.

NUTRITIONAL NOTES
PER PORTION:
CALORIES 191 PROTEIN 3.09g
FAT 6.26g SATURATED FAT 1.59g
CARBOHYDRATE 32.57g FIBER 1.66g
ADDED SUGAR 10.14g SODIUM 0.11g

COOK'S TIP
Rolled oats can be used in place of muesli for a delicious alternative.

INDEX